Diary of a
Farmer's Daughter

by Olga Onyschuk-Coleman-Doughty

To MARK
a friend of money
years lives perogies
& cabbage rolls

6/8/14

Produced by:

FriesenPress

Suite 300 – 852 Fort Street
Victoria, BC, Canada V8W 1H8

www.friesenpress.com

Distributed to the trade by The Ingram Book Company

Table of Contents

Preface

This book is based on the life experiences of the writer and these occurred in the workforce, in her travels and through her personal life.

After joining the workforce, her opinions on many things changed. It was her understanding that every workplace had their own standards that were supposed to be followed by the management level individuals as they were the team leaders and that incumbents would be treated fairly and respectively.

As time went on she found the attitudes displayed by supervisors and management staff were often unacceptable. There is good and bad in everyone as we are human and all make mistakes but we must also account for the misdoings. If everyone was perfect, what a perfect world we would have.

There are two sides to a coin and there are two sides to each issue. Through her experiences the management did not always want to hear your side and based their decisions on their own opinions. As a result some incumbents were denied raises and promotions. Often promotions were given to the wrong people who did not deserve them.

When she was growing up, she was taught "do onto others as you wish to be done to you". She found in almost all her jobs, favoritism played a big part in the workforce and this created poor morale and difficulties in the communication at the office. In some cases the problems were duplicated instead of being resolved.

It appeared that some individuals with a title of seniority did not always support their incumbents. They were impartial when attempting to resolve problems /issues, as a result the incumbents felt intimidated.

Often people were given management positions that they were not capable of handling and lacked the skills required. Instead of using constructive criticism, they chose to do the opposite and as a result the incumbents ended up with negative results.

After a number of years with a big firm, she felt harassment existed and decided to take the bull by the horns as the managers and junior supervisors did not always play by the rules. Even though, she was able to prove her case, it wasn't a victory for her. Weeks/months later, she encountered humiliation, intimidation, retaliation and blocked promotions, all because she tried to prove a point.

For personal reasons, she chose not to walk way. This career left her fighting for her rights on many occasions. She was determined to achieve her goals because she wasn't a quitter.

As the saying goes the grass always looks greener on the other side and sometimes it helps when you use a little sugar instead of salt, it sweetens the pot.

Whether you are rich or poor, you should always make the best of what life offers.

Introduction

This is a true story about a young lady who grew up on a farm under sheltered conditions and did not stray away from home until finishing grade twelve in a small town school. In her early years, the community life was simple; no TV and no special concessions. Friends, neighbors, and relatives were like one big happy family helping each other, and showing respect and compassion.

Throughout her years in the workforce, she came across situations where management personnel were not prepared to offer encouragement or show respect when it was needed.

In spite of the hardships endured (which she was able to overcome) she managed to stay with her second-last employer 6 years and 8 months, then tried to move up the ladder and joined another firm for over 20 years before retiring from the firm. She continued to work another 2 years for a small firm before that office closed doors and moved to a new city.

The experiences are based on true facts, ONLY the names have been changed to protect the identities and places.

The illustration for the book was designed by her nephew; Stuart N. Prysunka, Sherwood Park, Ab.

Chapter One

On July 23, 1939, God blessed two lucky parents (Mike and Mary), with a bouncing little girl who was welcomed into this world by her 2 brothers and 5 sisters, who came before her to check out the place. Her family accepted her graciously, with a brother and sister to follow, which completed the family circle.

Out of the 10 siblings, she was the first to be born in a hospital. The older ones were born at the homestead. She weighed more than 8 lbs at birth and complications arose. That meant she was born strong, with thick skin and ready to meet the world. God put us on this earth for a purpose, and when our job is done, we will be returned to him as angels; meaning our task never ends.

All the little people come into this world like innocent lambs, but what happens throughout their life is what really matters. Sometimes these lambs are used, abused and discriminated against. There is certainly no anticipation that they will experience torment through their lives, but how is one to know what the future holds in store for each and everyone.

This Is My Story

Our family consisted of twelve people and my parents raised 10 healthy children with three sisters departing at a ripe old age due to illness, and my parents have also gone to their resting place. Our mother was in her 70's, father in his 80's and the third-youngest sister in her 70's. It seems their duties had been completed and now they were called back. The oldest sister has now joined them at the age of 91 and the second oldest in 2013 in her 90's.

There certainly was no favoritism in our family just traditions. The other kids usually got the new stuff and the younger the hand-me-downs, but no one complained. We accepted life as it was in those days.

The rich had a specialty dish called "pheasant under glass". Our specialty was having partridge with creamed potatoes and wild mushrooms. It was best to pick these mushrooms after a hard rain. This was a specialty dish our parents and all of us enjoyed on special occasions.

Growing up on the farm also meant doing chores on a regular basis and everyone pitched in. At the age of 12, I had plenty of chores before leaving for school, like milking cows, feeding pigs and chickens. Our meat and milk products came off the farm.

After doing chores we walked to school several miles each day both ways. We often took shortcuts through the neighbors' fields to save time, but in the winter, we used a one-horse sled.

In those days we attended a one-room school with grades one to seven. After the seventh grade, we were transported to another school, in the town of Myrnam, and I attended school there until grade eleven.

The Junior High School was located in a small town close to the farming area and across a river. In the summer we crossed by ferry and in winter drove across the ice.

We had no school buses in those days, so we were transported to school usually in a small van. It had limited windows and was often crowded, but we managed. The town folks were always very friendly and some of the people I knew still live there. The school still exists and is being used by the new generations.

A new school was built south of the farm in the town of St. Paul, and all the students going into grade twelve then moved to this new location. I graduated from this school (Glen Avon) along with my schoolmates who lived in the same farming community.

After moving to the new school, I needed extra funds for clothing and books. I chose to work part time and moved in with my sister and her family. In return, I helped out with housework and babysitting. I befriended a family who owned a hotel and they hired me in the restaurant as a waitress. I worked after school and week-ends. Sometimes my sister worked shifts for me when I had extra homework.

The picture of me and my schoolmates graduating hung proudly on the hallway wall. I was certainly proud to be one of the first to graduate from this new school. The school has moved to another area of town. The building is being used for college students as the town is too small to have a College.

Many relatives still attend the same school, mostly my nieces' and nephews' children. Going to College or University in those days was out of the question. First of all, my parents did not have the funds for schooling, and secondly very high marks were required to meet the standards of these schools.

My only alternative was to look for work, save up some funds, and return to school at a future date. With the bankroll being low, I went job hunting and was prepared to take what I could get. Even though I often thought about returning, I never managed to return to College or University on a full time basis but I did take some night courses.

Growing up we experienced a lot of good memories on the farm, which the seniors sometimes referred to as the good old days. Each Christmas when the family gathered, we shared the traditional twelve dishes of our nationality for our meal. Our tree decorations were made at home. We made popcorn strings, picked pine cones and occasionally had a bought decoration. The "good old days" seemed to have been less stressful.

We may have been poor folks living in a rich man's world but celebrated life the best we knew how. We never experienced violence or the child abuse that goes on in this century now. We were happy to crowd around a radio and listen to music or news of the world.

It was very entertaining to us at that time. Now, the younger generation only wants computers, ipads, iphones, and watching TV on big screens and listening to loud music. They even use calculators to do simple additions, while we did everything manually and survived.

After the Christmas meal, the adults sat around the heater (people now have fireplaces), told jokes and talked about many things. The young people either went tobogganing or used the home-made sleds, and took turns going down the big hill in front of our house.

Even though our sleds were made by our dad along with everything else, we seemed to manage and also things were cheaper. He warned us about touching the hard stuff but my younger brother and I decided to experiment. It turned out we slept most of the next two days after that experience.

Our Christmas gifts were very traditional. Each year we received a new pair of shoes, boots or clothing that was needed. Our mother prepared little surprise packages with oranges, nuts and candy. This was special to us and we looked forward to it each year.

In this day and age, many children hardly know their parents, mainly because they grow up in daycare centers from an early age. With both parents working, who is teaching the kids right from wrong?? Most children fend for themselves before and after school. As they grow older they become very independent and uncontrollable.

Since we had a huge front yard, in the summer the neighbors gathered at our house and we learned to play softball now known as fastball. We removed grass to mark the bases and the bats were homemade. The game was enjoyed by all the participants.

Our mother always grew a large garden and loved flowers everywhere. Each year after the garden was planted she would spread poppy seeds on the whole garden, as the flowers started to bloom, the garden looked like Flanders' field with the red poppies. We used the poppy seeds for baking and poppy seed cakes became one of our favorite pastries.

As kids, we would eat the poppy seeds right of the garden because they were harmless and a special treat to us. To this day we are still big on poppy seed cake and a favorite of many.

We lived off our produce on the farm. Vegetables and berries were canned. We made our own butter and even ice cream, which was limited. Our meat came from pigs and cows. Our dad made homemade sausage for us.

We also raised chickens and turkeys. We often tried to tease the turkeys and got bit. One of our daily chores was collecting the eggs. Our mother always baked bread and buns. As we got older we all pitched in and helped with garden work, cooking, baking, laundry and other chores.

Being Ukrainian, we grew up on perogies, cabbage rolls and enjoyed many other favorite dishes. Every year we pickled cucumbers and made mustard pickles. We learned to enjoy pickle and peanut butter sandwiches and still eat them to this day.

Berry picking was a big chore for us each summer, as many families canned or stored them for the winter months. The whole family became involved when it came to berry picking, the old and the young with everyone enjoying it.

We had a favorite saying at the area where we did most of the berry picking. It was "Get your thrill on Blueberry Hill". We picked blueberries, cranberries, saskatoon berries and pinchherries. We used the berries for baking and making jams and jellies, which usually lasted throughout the winter months. Then the next summer we did it again.

We lived on home grown food which kept us healthy and active. These days in the big cities, everything we buy is made by someone else, or at least most of it is. Few people grow their own.

When we had colds, our mom made us eat onion sandwiches, sometimes with added oranges, and used mustard packs on our chests. For cuts and bruises she picked special mushrooms, dried them and used the powder. These home treatments seemed to work. Medications were seldom used, and there were also Watkins products, which came along gradually.

Like most kids we weren't always angels and were naughty on occasion. Our neighbors often went berry picking with us or on their own. When they went on their own, they often stopped to visit with our parents and had lunch and tea. While they enjoyed their tea at our house, we enjoyed sampling their pickings and lightening their load a bit.

They may have not noticed, but our parents always knew, sometimes they made us go pick some extra berries and deliver to our neighbors. Only then they realized what had happened, however, there were never hard feelings.

There was only one Post Office in a small village where the farm people got their mail. Since it was a very long walk, every Saturday two of us would pack a lunch and hike to pick up the mail.

Life seemed so simple at that time and finances were not so complicated. Now you almost need several jobs to make ends meet and often they don't. The cost of living has certainly gone up and a lot people are unemployed due to many layoffs. Things have really changed.

My younger sister and I learned to ride a horse at an early age. My parents always owned some tame horses. These horses were often slow and too old to run fast, so they were suitable for us. My sister and I would jump on one of the horses and go for a ride bareback, as we had no fear of falling off at that age and did not use saddles.

The roads had a lot of sand and it did not hurt much when we did accidentally fall off. My sister was approx. 5 years old then and I wasn't much older. We slid off the horse a few times as he or she rounded the corner, as we only had the horse's mane to hang on to. The horses always came back after they dumped us and never let us down.

After leaving the farm and going to the city, I still enjoyed horseback riding and continued going on trail rides for several years with friends. On one trail ride, the horse I was riding decided he needed to cool off while crossing a small creek with less than 3 feet of water.

This horse decided he would go down and get me soaked to the skin. I wasn't afraid of falling, but I certainly did not want to get wet. Needless to say I never rode him again.

They always had a wiener roast after the ride and I sat by the fire hoping my clothes would dry off before we left for home. The ranch hands were always helpful and gave me some dry clothes to wear home that day.

The older sisters left the farm at an early age and the younger siblings helped with the farm work.

New land cleared for seeding usually contained rocks that would damage machinery. We had a platform drawn by a horse (known as a stoneboat) on which we loaded the rocks and disposed of them.

When grain was cut, we stacked the sheaves so the grain would dry faster. At harvest, we delivered meals to the farm hands.

Chapter Two

In 1958 after leaving high school and graduating from grade twelve, I landed my first job in the work force. It was at a local hospital which was run by an Order of Sisters in the town of Vegreville, close to our town.

I was offered an opportunity to enter the workforce, even though, I had no experience. I accepted the position in the Medical Records Department. There, I learned a lot about health problems and illnesses that existed and how they were treated.

The income offered was limited and expenses were high, but I managed to survive on what I had. Being raised on a farm taught me many things, you do not take things for granted and you have to work for what you want.

Clothes were expensive then as they are now. I made my own clothes for years after taking sewing and knitting lessons at night school. Often I even sewed for others or knitted items I could sell or give away as gifts. I learned how to cut expenses and still managed to support myself from the age of 18, as my family was not well off. You did what you needed to do to survive without their help.

After working for several months at this medical facility, I was offered another position at a Sisters facility with more opportunities as the Sisters looked after their people. The other facility required students who were willing to train as a nurse's aide, and eventually graduate to become a nurse if they chose to do so.

It was suggested to me that I should take the training, and if at a later date I chose to not continue, I could always change to something else. I decided to challenge this opportunity, with possibilities for advancement.

At the new hospital in Lethbridge, the Sisters were helpful at giving instructions and advice. The nurse's aide positions were promoted as they were greatly needed at hospitals. I was shown a lot of respect, but after a number of months, I realized this was not the career path I wanted to take. I discussed this with the Sister in charge who was disappointed but offered me several other positions in the hospital.

I spent a short period of time in the Pathology Lab, but this position did not appeal to me. Then I accepted a position in the emergency department and worked on the switchboard. I enjoyed working on the switchboard but seeing the people in the trauma center was heart breaking. If you have ever been at a scene of an accident with injuries, you will know what situations I encountered on a daily basis.

I enjoyed this department but it was getting stressful. It was disappointing to know life was so short for these unfortunate individuals and my heart went out to those who suffered with illness or loss. The victims of hunting accidents were hard to face.

After leaving that department, I accepted a position in the Admitting Office, facing many different situations. I dealt with sick children, seniors and new mothers who had to be rushed to maternity.

I almost had to deliver a baby on the elevator because the baby decided it was time. The best part of this position was seeing the newborns, when registering their names and sometimes you were allowed to cuddle them.

In July of 1960, before we left the hospital, I decided to go on a camping trip with a family, whom I had room and boarded with, when first coming to work at the hospital. Later on I got my own apartment. I had never camped before and did not know what to expect.

I wasn't aware at the time but I think they asked me to join them so I could help pay for the trip. I ended up paying for my share and some of their expenses. They borrowed funds, promised to pay back but never did.

The first night we stayed at a campground located near a small beach at Waterton Lakes. The mother of a family tenting next to us was taking her kids to the swimming pool and invited us along, so we joined them. The next day we moved to the campground inside the park.

We were warned about bears in the area but never expected to see any. While out walking, we spotted a brown bear at a distance and made a quick exit back to camp. We befriended a couple of RCMP who posed for pictures at that park and we had some interesting conversations.

We visited Cameron Lake and the Red Rock Canyon. The weather was really warm and sometimes up to 90 degrees Fahrenheit. Then, 4 days later the muffler fell off, so the parents went into town while I watched their kids at the campsite. The next day we continued on and crossed at "Chief Mountain Customs". They asked questions at the border but we did not run into any problems.

We passed through Babb, Montana before heading into Glacier Park. Our next stop was St. Mary's Lake. We saw Red Eagle Mountain with an elevation of 8850 ft. We stopped at Florence Falls, passed the Jackson Glacier then stopped at Mount Jackson (elevation 10,033 ft.) for a short time.

The vehicle overheated, and we stopped to cool it off. The temperature was 100 degrees Fahrenheit, no wonder the vehicle over-heated, and we had travelled a lot of miles without stopping.

After the vehicle cooled off, we continued through Logan Pass (6664 ft.), Bird Woman Falls in Oberlin, MT., and on to the Glacier Park campground. On the way there we saw a black mother bear and her young cub on the roadside. Many people stopped to take pictures.

The Avalanche Campground was where most people stayed. There were camp tables near the office. A family was having their picnic when 3 young black bears came by. The family got up and stood back. The bears took what they wanted and left. This reminded me of Goldie Locks and the 3 bears.

After registering at this campsite, we were advised that there were bears wondering around this park. They said as long as the food was locked up in the trunk or a safe place the bears would not bother you. It seemed a bit scary but we stayed anyway.

I ended up with an abscess tooth and the only medication I had was aspirin. I crushed the tablet and covered my tooth to help with the pain. After setting up camp, we realized there was a tire problem. The nearest garage was 12 miles away, so the parents drove there to get it fixed before it got dark.

Their tent was not big enough to hold the whole family, so one of the girls and I stayed in a pup tent. It didn't seem very safe with all the bears around. The people in a tent next to us about 6-7 feet away, went to a friend's place for the night and left the tent unattended.

The next morning when we got up, we found their tent torn to shreds. There were young black bears all around the tent, one in a tree and several in the tent checking it out. These cubs were possibly 2-3 years old and the mother was not in sight. We did nothing and stayed in our tents until they left.

We found out later that one of the kids left part of a banana in the tent and the bears smelled it. It was too close for comfort so we checked out and moved on. We went past Kalispell, Hungry Horse Dam, several Memorial Parks, the Trap Zoo, and ended up camping at Flathead Lake.

It was now July 23 and we were heading to Spokane where I hoped to spend my 21 birthday, but it was too far to travel in one day. We checked out a few campgrounds along the way but they were booked. When we stopped for gas at one of the stations (gas was $.31 a gallon plus tax – $.08), the attendant was able to refer us to a campground where we could stop for the night in Albertan, Mont.

The next morning after breakfast we were on our way into the Idaho State, known for their potatoes, as we passed the Idaho State line, the elevation was 4738 feet. We, also, went past many coal mines. Then we went though Wallace, Osburn, Elk Creek and Kellogg, ending up at Coeur d'Alene, where we camped for the night. After travelling 300 miles that day, we were all very tired and needed a break.

By the time we got to Spokane, I did not feel like celebrating, as the toothache got worse, and I had some swelling on my face. I decided to deal with my tooth when I got home and aspirin would have to do in the meantime, but I wasn't a happy camper. I remember travelling down Sprague, which they claimed was the longest avenue in Spokane. The parents wanted me to have a beer since I just turned 21, but with my toothache I turned it down. They had no problem celebrating on my behalf.

We headed next to Davenport, Grand Coulee Dam, and passed through Wilbur and Creston, which was still in Washington, stayed on the US side for the night and headed into B.C. the next day. We entered at the South Okanagan Valley through Omak and crossed the Okanagan River. We went through Tonasket and Orville, spending the night at Osoyoos Lake.

After going through customs, we went through Bridesville and Kettle River. Then we passed through Grand Forks and Deadman's Creek, crossed the Columbia River and on to Trail. We set up the last camp at Balfour, B.C. before I took a bus home, as I had to return to work, and the rest carried on with their trip.

After spending several years at this facility, another co-worker and I decided we needed a change and wanted to try new challenges.

As most of our experience was obtained at this one facility, we knew that we would have to learn other professions. Margie (my co-worker) suggested we move to the big neighboring city as it was large and should have many opportunities.

In the fall of 1960, we gave our notice, packed our bags and headed for the big city known the Cow Town of the west (Calgary), and rodeos were held there annually. The bright lights impressed us a great deal as we had never seen this before. The buildings were not very tall and there were no one-way streets at that time.

Having no vehicles, we walked a lot, and used public transportation once in a while, but it was limited. We often walked 10 or more blocks, one way, and then back the same distance.

We located a small basement suite in a private residence, and felt it would do until we managed to find work. Jobs were limited for people with our experience. Our first jobs were waitress jobs, which we didn't mind, as we needed an income.

After awhile, we realized, this wasn't what we wanted to do on a full time basis. We encountered many different experiences with the clientele. Some showed respect, while others were sometimes very rude, demanding and tipped little.

Our landlord had two small children and often we babysat for them. The basement was renovated into two one-bedroom suites. The second suite was rented to another female tenant. She worked shift work so we did not see her much. Margie and I decided we would share a suite until we had better incomes, then if we chose to do so we would get our own places later on.

The landlord was very trusting and did something he should not have. One Sunday morning when we decided to sleep in, something strange happened in our building. The boyfriend of the girl in the next suite to ours was looking to surprise her on her birthday.

He planned to cook her breakfast while she was in bed. The landlord misunderstood and assumed that he was looking for us. He let the gentleman in without our knowledge which was a stupid thing to do. In those days crime was not as bad but still some people could not or should not be trusted.

Margie was first to get up that morning and thought it was strange that she smelled bacon cooking in our kitchen. She knew it wasn't me cooking and for a short moment she panicked. She quickly woke me up and we approached the kitchen with extreme caution not knowing what to expect.

As we approached the kitchen, to our surprise, we saw a guy cooking breakfast (little did we know he was a chef) in our kitchen, and it scared us. When he saw us, he was just as shocked as us, if not more.

He apologized over and over again for the mistake as he was totally embarrassed. He explained that he thought he was in his girlfriend's apartment, and wanted to cook her breakfast. Since he had already cooked breakfast, we invited her over and we ate together.

All went well that day, but we informed the landlord that this was not a good thing he did, and not to ever do this again. The person could have been dangerous, and wanted to enter for a different reason. For all the time we lived there, we never encountered anything like this again and we never had breakfast cooked for us either.

After working several months as waitresses, completing numerous resumes and applications, an ad appeared in the local paper which stated the firm was looking for a receptionist. The position was open for a person who was familiar with medical terms, and could deal with clientele who experienced some financial hardships due to a lot of medical bills that incurred.

I decided to apply, as I felt it could be up my alley and a chance to get into a different workforce. In January, 1961, after the interview, I was offered the position. It turned out to be a small collection office, that handled delinquent accounts in the medical field.

As a general clerk, I would be answering the phone, completing insurance claims, sending out billings, and other miscellaneous duties. It wasn't a high-paying job, but it was an income. Margie also obtained new employment. We got our own apartments but kept in touch.

The office was located in the heart of downtown and I could walk to work. The manager of the office was Garth. He was friendly but we soon found out he worked his staff hard. He had his ways of doing things and he often let you know in front of other co-workers.

His management skills were not always the best, but he managed to collect the debts outstanding for his clients. Often his attitude needed adjusting as he did not always treat others well. Soon the office morale seemed to go down, and staff slowly departed one by one, finding other positions. I decided to make the move in the fall of 1963.

After several interviews, I decided to seek employment with another financial firm, "Castle Credit and Collections". A friend suggested that there may be more opportunities and advancement there, even though the position open was only for a receptionist.

It was a small office, but had a friendly atmosphere from the first appearance, and had limited staff. They needed a receptionist, so they offered me the position. I was looking forward to the challenge. The hours were 9-5 daily and no overtime which suited me.

After a short period of time, I transferred to the loan department, as a loan officer and a collector. I learned from the beginning the firm was aggressive in the business, and expected everyone to give it a 100% to meet their goals.

Most people had two incomes when they borrowed and based their budget on that. Then when one party got laid off, or there was illness in the family and only one income, problems began and sometimes were hard to handle.

At one point I felt confident that I could handle this line of work with the experience I already had. Every new position had challenging aspects, you need to give it your best shot and not give up.

Usually the minority groups do the manual work (at that time there were no computers), and don't get credit for it or rewarded for their good deeds. It seems the credit usually goes to the management personnel.

Since I had just moved to a new basement suite, my youngest brother who was working in Williams Lake, BC on a ranch, decided he wanted to come and visit me. He loved horses and participated in small rodeos. The prizes weren't big at that time but he enjoyed it. I still have a cowboy hat he won at one of the rodeos.

I encouraged him to come for the Stampede, so in July, 1964, he came and spent a week with me. We took in the Stampede activities and he toured the city a bit. We played some games at the stampede grounds, and I won an orange and white teddy bear which I still have 49 years later.

One of the co-workers from the previous job and I became good friends. Shelley suggested we go a vacation via a tour bus and see other places. We checked out the tours and found one we thought we would like. However, it meant spending a lot of time on the road and sleeping on the bus on occasion. The bus was equipped for long trips and had a washroom. We were naïve about travelling but we were willing to challenge it.

On Aug. 7, 1964 we boarded the bus and headed for Fort MacLeod, then stopped for lunch in Fernie, B.C. We arrived in Creston at 5:30 am, had breakfast and headed across the border into the USA. We went through Idaho State by passing Bonner's Ferry, Naples, Sandpoint, and stopped for a short time in Coeur d'Alene.

When we got to Spokane, we had a 2-hour stop for lunch and a change of drivers. As we passed through the small towns, the bus driver gave us the names and important points. It was now the 8th of Aug. as we entered Oregon and saw the Umatilla Air Base. The bus continued through Rufus, by the Johnbay Dam, the Dalles Bus Depot, and on to Portland, arriving there at 10:20 pm. We stayed on the 9th floor at the Heathman's Hotel. The next morning, after leaving Portland with a new driver, we stopped at Taft to have lunch and continued on to California.

We were advised to bring snacks along on the bus. At some of the bus depots there were no places to get food and only one washroom in the whole place with constant lineups. We changed drivers again and went on to Eureka, arriving at 9:30 pm. tired and hungry.

We walked 4 blocks to our hotel from the bus depot, and then 8 blocks to a restaurant. There wasn't much to do in the area so we went to bed early. The next day we headed to San Francisco with a new driver arriving there at 3:30 pm and spent several days there.

Our hotel was not fancy but we toured others in the area. One was 19 stories and the other 24, and since I did not like heights, I stayed away from the windows. The one with 24 stories had a glass elevator outside the building which I rode up, as I had no choice. The restaurant was on the 24th floor and we chose to eat there.

We went to the Bumble Bee Club and the Franco's Club. We stood at the door when we entered the second club and saw girls on the stage singing and dancing. There were a lot of male clientele around the stage. We soon realized this wasn't for us and left. The cover charge for this club was $1.65, drinks $1.00, and beer was only $.50 at that time.

The bellboy was concerned that we might go to the wrong places that were unsafe for females and volunteered to be our guide while we were there. He even gave us a list of places we could go on our own.

We visited Fisherman's Wharf and had lunch there, but did not like the smell of fish everywhere. The next day, we left for Los Angeles. We went pass the State

College and the Ford Motor Plant. This plant covered 280 acres. We were booked at the Mayfair Hotel on the 10th floor, and decided to stay in and relax that night.

The next day the tour bus took us to Disneyland at 9:30 am. Our tour guide Kathy was very helpful with information. This park was completed in 1954 and officially opened to the public in 1955. It was situated on 67 acres and the parking lot on 105 acres. It could accommodate 61,000 visitors at one time. The admission to the park was $5.00. On July 4, 1964, records show 60,917 people visited the park.

We rode the train on the Santa Fe Railway, visited Frontier land, saw Swiss Robinson tree, Adventure land, Tom Sawyer Island, Fantasy Land, rode the Monorail, and saw much more. We saw the famous Wax Museum of the Hollywood Stars and Knott's Berry Farm. We were told at that time this farm grossed approximately 17 million a year because of tourism.

We spent the next day shopping close to the hotel, used the swimming pool, and saw a movie (Good Neighbor Sam). The following day we toured Universal Studios with a new bus driver, who was also the tour guide. He advised us, the population of Los Angeles was 2,753,300, and the area was 473 square miles. It had 126 parks and playgrounds.

On the way there we went past San Fernando Valley and Burbank. The population of Burbank was 81,000 and it had 5 studios which included Walt Disney, NBC and Columbia.

Our next tour began with the residential area of the movie stars: Bing Crosby's first home, Jeff Chandler's, Bob Hope's new and old, and the honeymoon home of

Eddie and Debbie Fisher plus many others. We were not allowed in the homes, but could view from the outside and take pictures.

Then, we entered north Hollywood and Universal Studios which was located on 750 acres. They showed us dressing rooms, storage area, filming areas and the homes they used in various shows.

The popular shows at that time were Virginian, Wagon Train, Leave it to Beaver, To Kill a Mocking Bird, Monsters, McHale's Navy, PT109, High Noon (Gary Cooper), and my favorite: Bonanza (Lorne Green). We actually watched a segment of the show was being filmed, and were close enough to some of the actors to say a few words to them. The Bonanza house was also used for the film Psycho. We also saw Tony Curtis' Rolls Royce.

Leaving there, we travelled down Hollywood Blvd saw more homes and the Chinese Theatre where the footprints of movie stars were. The tour continued by Capital Records, Hollywood Palace Theater and by Paramount Studios/ KTTV Television Studio. This studio was purchased by Gene Autry at the time for 12 million.

It is Aug. 18th and we are now heading for Las Vegas. We decided we needed to spruce up a bit and attended the Hairdresser Shop in the hotel. They touched up our hair for $2.00, unbelievable with the prices these days. We were then set to check out the clubs.

We didn't gamble much, but managed to win $40.00, which was a lot at that time. We took in the Horseshoe Casino, The Mint, Vegas Club, Golden Nugget, The Jackpot, the California Club, and many others. We took in some of the live entertainment and listened to several singers we knew.

We left Vegas and headed for Salt Lake City, travelled through St George, Utah and arrived at our destination by 10:00 pm. It was not a nice hotel, but it was okay for one night. Next morning we did a bit of touring, saw the Mormon Temple and were on our way through Idaho. We passed through the towns of Ogden, Logan, Cedar City, and Idaho Falls. We stopped for lunch and headed for Montana. We were homeward bound.

We had a 2 hour stop in Great Falls, cleared customs in Sweet Grass, crossed Coutts border, went through Warner, Lethbridge, Fort MacLeod, and arrived home that night at 5:30 pm. It turned out to be a great experience and the beginning of a great friendship.

After the trip we vowed to keep in touch and remain friends. Later, Shelley introduced me to several of her friends, Glenda and Deana. The four of us became good friends and still remain as friends, but socialize less now. Some of my friends lost their spouses and have found new things to do. We still make time to have dinner together occasionally.

While working at the hospital, I purchased a (black and white) TV. I was told the amount could be repaid in monthly installments but I was not told that there were extra charges when paying on time. I guess I didn't ask the right questions. It was the first time I bought an item on credit.

I would not have signed a contract had I known about the charges and would have paid cash. The biggest thing that upset me was the 24% charge which I wasn't prepared to pay. After a number of discussions they agreed to negotiate the charge and I paid them out.

Nowadays, many people do not worry about paying charges, as long as they can have the item in their possession.

Of course, even if you do grow up on the farm, you know you have to work for your income. Also on a farm your income comes different sources like raising cattle or growing grains and vegetables that later be sold or taking on jobs as farmhands.

This young girl growing up on Blueberry Hill was learning the facts of life sooner than she anticipated. Working at the hospital was not a big paying job but it was challenging and I learned that I had to budget my pay in order to be able to pay my expenses on time.

In the summer of 1966, my sister's young boys decided they wanted to visit me as they heard about the great Stampede. They were 10 and 12, and were old enough to ride on the bus by themselves so their mother sent them to this fine city. I met my nephews at the bus depot and they spent a week with me. It was their first trip on their own to a big city. They will always treasure this experience and still talk about it.

They arrived a day before the stampede, so we got up early the next morning to attend the famous parade. That year some of the special guests were Robert and Ethel Kennedy, Red Adair and Burl Ives. At the grounds they enjoyed playing some games, touring the buildings and most enjoyed the Big Four Building. There were many items displayed there that they had never seen before.

They also visited the Zoo and the Glenbow Museum which they greatly enjoyed. We mostly used the bus as transportation and sometimes we walked depending where we went. Although my income was limited at the time we managed well. We usually packed lunches and drinks from home and used the extra funds for activities they wanted to partake. Some evenings we took in movies that they wanted to see. Their younger brother designed the illustration for my book.

I wasn't exactly the athletic type and all activities cost to participate in, so I budgeted accordingly. I took up bowling, played softball, took in a few shows, and horseback riding. I played Bingo occasionally, won some, and lost some, but it was an outing and I made some new friends.

In the fall of 1967, my younger sister and her friend decided to go to Phoenix, Az. Her friend's mom felt they should not venture out alone and requested that an adult accompany them. Since I had already travelled a bit, she requested I join them on this trip.

At first I didn't think I could get time off, and I had worked for a long time without a vacation. I found that I really needed a break, so I arranged for time off. We went shopping, bought new suits, packed our bags and headed out. We looked like three office girls on a business trip with our new attire.

We were able to arrange an excellent travel package. At the hotel, they gave us a bigger room with 3 single beds so we could all stay together. Since it wasn't their busy season, they were happy to accommodate our needs.

In our package was included a rental car. Budget-rent-a-car met us at the airport and gave us a 1967 Olds. We had to pay the insurance and gas expenses. We did a lot of touring in the area and spent a lot of time at a lake nearby.

One day while at the lake, we ended up with a flat tire. It was really fortunate we met someone that was willing to help us. But a few hours later, again we had a flat tire, so we called the rental firm and requested a different car.

My sister did most of the driving as she had driven more. Since we had some transportation, we decided to do some touring on our own and felt Tucson would be a good place to visit.

The three of us got into the car and took off. When we got to Tucson, her friend needed something from the pharmacy and wanted me to go get it. They agreed to drive around the block and pick me up. I got out of the car but did not take my purse or anything else except a $10.00 bill and was only wearing shorts and a T-shirt as it was terribly hot that day.

After making the purchase I stepped outside and waited, but there was no sign of them. So I waited and waited. I still did not see them, wondering where they could be. About now I was starting to panic because I had no ID on me and no money, other than the change of the $10.00.

They must have driven by at least ten times before they recognized the place where they dropped me off. Finally I was able to flag them down. New rule: we stick together no matter where we go and were prepared if by some chance we separated.

A few days later on our trip from the lake, my sister got a ticket for speeding as we were too busy talking. We left the lake still partly in our bathing suits so when the police stopped us they gave us a hard time about the clothing.

At the time the speeding tickets were set for $1.00 per mile over the speed limit. The ticket was to be paid immediately at a judge's office. The officer gave us directions to get there. When we got there the office was closed. Just our luck, the sign said to come back at 8:00 am.

There wasn't much we could do that night. We went back to the hotel, had a drink and played pool with some of the pilots staying at the hotel whom we made friends with and stuck around the hotel.

We got up early the next morning and headed to the judge's office as the ticket needed to be paid between 8-10 am, otherwise they arrest you. The fine was $25.00 and we chipped in and paid it.

When we got back to the hotel, we were informed to be on the lookout and not stray too far from the hotel. A prisoner escaped from a Tucson prison, killed a guard and apparently held a woman as a hostage, but she was not harmed. Other news we were given was that, there was a hurricane in another part of the USA and two other people were found dead in Tucson.

At the hotel they offered tours to Las Vegas so the three naïve girls boarded a bus and headed for Nevada. We also managed to see the Hoover Dam. It was a day trip and pretty tiring. Due to the unexciting news received previously, we mostly hung around the hotel area for the next week.

I don't know if it was being naïve or stupid that made us do what we did. We were determined to have a good time. Not being big travelers, we were not aware we needed passports go to Mexico, as no passports were required to enter USA.

We got into our rented car and headed for Nogales, Mexico. We crossed the border in the car before realizing it was a no-no.

The first thing that happened was, we locked the keys in the car and the border guard says no problem. He called a locksmith who came in his van. As he opened the door of the van we saw he had hundreds of keys to open cars. We worried about leaving the car there but the guard said it was okay.

After a bit of shopping we decided to head back to Phoenix and that is when our problems began. By then the border guards changed and when we tried to cross back, they wanted us to produce passports or they weren't going to let us go back. We knew we were in trouble.

However, after searching every inch of the car, all our belongings, checking our ID's, and with our pleading they agreed to let us head back. They warned us about coming back without passports.

We never ventured to another town again without checking things out first. We returned to our hotel and spent a few more days there then headed for home. It turned out to be an experience of a life time and we will always cherish the memories.

Chapter Three

After leaving the previous employment I was befriended by a guy that worked at the bank where I did my personal banking. He had recently moved to Canada from England and knew only a few people. Travis and I started spending time together and eventually it got more serious.

After a period of courting we decided to get married in August of 1969. The wedding was held at the town I came from so it would be easier for my family to attend, as I came from a large family. His family was small and several relatives came from England.

We travelled a bit by going to the USA and Mexico, spent some time in Acapulco and New Mexico where we got badly sunburned but survived. We spent too much time in the sun on the beach without sunscreen. The next couple of days we basically hung around the hotel.

We were warned by several people we befriended, to be careful about any purchases we made. After you pay for your item, they reach for a bag under the counter and switch the merchandise. We were told to always check your bag before leaving the cashier. I purchased a leather purse and double checked before I left in front of them.

We also decided to head to England so I could meet his relatives and friends there. One of his friends still keeps in touch even though we are no longer together. Since we travelled to England in the month of February, the weather was chilly.

His brother picked us up at the airport, and half way home the car broke down. Some residents in the area assisted and we stayed with them until new transportation arrived. When we got to his mother's house, it was warmer outside then inside.

By then I had already acquired a cold so they warmed up the bed with pans that had long handles and water bottles. I tried to warm up in bed, but my cold persisted and lasted for some time. It was nice and cozy when you were in bed but cold when you got out because the whole house was chilly. The bathroom was huge with no heat, and the window was open. Each room was heated separately.

We travelled also to visit other relatives in Scotland. There was also limited heat there. The bathroom was large and hard to heat so we had to wash up in the chilly room. I knew in February they had snow, but I did not realize how much.

In the morning when we woke up we couldn't go anywhere to tour because it had snowed a lot. We could not get out of the yard let alone drive on the road. We had to wait for the snow plow to clear the roads.

I survived the trip to England and Wales and was able to see Buckingham Palace from outside the fence. The next day we were fortunate to see the Queen and Princess Anne up close as they were going by in a carriage.

However, I found their cooking was different and they shopped daily for fresh veggies and bread.

I had Brussels sprouts mostly every day I was there as this was one of the cheapest vegetables. After a while I got tired of the vegetable but ate it anyway. When I returned to Canada, I could not even look at Brussels sprouts for a long time.

I did not like the way coffee was boiled and milk was added while still bubbling. I preferred to add milk once it cooled off a bit. Coffee was soon not my favorite drink while there, I mostly drank juices.

We ate a lot of eggs growing up and the eggs were cooked different ways but not like the ones in England. Whether they were scrambled, sunny side up or flipped over the whites on the eggs were not completely cooked. I found I could not eat them cooked this style. When I returned to Canada, it took me a long time to enjoy eating eggs again.

During this trip we had the opportunity to visit Holland, toured the famous Anne Frank house and some of the canals. We also visited my sister in Germany as her husband was stationed there with the Armed Forces.

While in Germany, I played a small slot machine in the pub for the fun of it. At first it paid very little but then it went wild and each time I put a coin in I got at least 10 or more out. The bar tender watched for a few minutes then he said, "machine broke", several times and would not let me play it anymore. I guess I emptied out most of the coins and he wasn't happy.

While spending time there, my sister and I decided to do the Paris scene. I always wanted to see the Eiffel Tower. It was interesting, and a bit scary on the trains, but we survived. We did get off once at the wrong stop but luckily a taxi took us to the right place. They asked for the passport at every stop.

When we got to Paris my sister said, "I would like to know what the folks in our home town are doing, here we are, two country bumpkins enjoying the likes of Paris, France." After returning to Germany I headed home.

As time went on Travis was getting bored with banking and decided to pursue a new a career. He, eventually, joined the police force. Having a spouse in the police force changes your life style. I did, however, enjoy the social events where I made friends.

Sometimes it was hard to co-ordinate events or outings as the new job involved shift work and a lot of involvement with the public. We befriended some couples and I kept in touch with the spouses. In this line of work it is very easy to be led astray because you meet a lot of different people.

Eventually he seemed to be working a lot of extra security duties which I thought was part of his job, and later found out that it wasn't the case from his partner. Unable to resolve our differences, we parted company and went our separate ways.

The firm I was working for did well at first. As time went on they felt the office was overstaffed and payroll decided changes had to be made. At the time the firm was not in a position to promote females to management and there was little advancement.

The staff got along well and we had many social events that were very enjoyable, but all good things come to an end. We were advised that in the fall of 1971, they had plans to close the office and move to another location. They planned to combine two offices in another city and would not be transferring any staff.

They advised that they would offer packages but if some chose to leave before the office closed they could. Some of the co-workers did find employment immediately and left. One of the co-workers, Blanche, and I decided to stay on but continued to look for other jobs. There wasn't much available and so we weren't in a big rush to take the first job.

After leaving the firm, Blanche and I decided to take a trip before taking on a new job. The severance pay they gave us covered us for a short while. Only the ones that stayed to the closing date received severance pay. We decided to spend some time in Kalispell, Montana.

The advantage of holidays is being able to sleep in but it also tends to make a person lazy at the best of times. We had just returned from the USA, where we spent time sun tanning, sightseeing and enjoyed the night life. It was nice to be home again, but it was also time to return to the working world.

I searched the ads daily and located a firm looking for a person with financial experience. I called them for more information. The company was doing wholesale financing for car dealers. I was ready to take on another financial firm and arranged an interview.

I attended the firm, Comstock Credit and was interviewed by the manager, Art. He explained what the position was about and I decided to accept. I hoped it would give me the opportunity to learn about wholesale and retail financing and maybe gain advancement.

He advised that they were short staffed, and we would be expected to work overtime when necessary. What he omitted to tell me, at the time, was he had no budget for overtime and not prepared to pay it. However, he still expected the assigned duties to be completed as requested.

Our hours were originally 9-5 for the first few months. As the workloads increased we ended up working to 6 or 7 pm. Sometimes we even came in an hour early. All the extra hours began stressing the co-workers out as everyone was completing extra duties. We often had to change planned holidays as per request of management.

We were not happy with this situation, so we arranged a meeting with the management to express our feelings, but that did not go over well. Art wasn't the easiest person to get along with, and his attitude was somewhat different, one minute he agreed with you, and the next he didn't. We were unable to work out an amicable arrangement.

He often set very high goals which were impossible to meet. Sometimes it was uncomfortable to work with him and still hold a smiling face. He also advised the staff if they did not like the working conditions they could leave.

One by one the staff slowly diminished, and each time someone left, the workload kept increasing. He did not hire new staff, just distributed that person's work among the staff left. I decided I would try to stick it out as long as I could.

Eventually one of the co-worker and I decided it was time to move on. We had gained enough knowledge and experience in this type of financing.

We felt that, if we were to buy a new vehicle, we would be able to determine if it was a good deal. At this point, we were able tell the difference between retail and wholesale.

Chapter Four

I had a lot of paid holidays stacked up, so when I resigned I took almost a month off and went on a short vacation before venturing into a new job. Upon my return I checked out some possible jobs.

It was a nice warm winter day in mid February-1973, the sun was shining, making it a perfect day for relaxing on the porch with a nice cold drink, but duty calls, bills must be paid and there were more important matters to deal with. I had an interview lined up for the next day and I was a bit nervous. Half asleep the next morning I stepped into the shower, hoping this would wake me up. As I dressed I felt wide awake, full of energy and ready to meet the day or whatever was in store.

Most of the previous firms, I worked for were not in the process of prompting women and their increases were minimal. I was hoping there would be more opportunity with my next job, as the previous could not offer any advancement.

With the cost of living going up, most people found it hard to make ends meet. Some stay-at-home moms were now starting to choose careers to help with family expenses. This is when daycare started to became very popular and the jobs became less available.

At that time, I was able to handle my finances and I continued to participate with sports activities to meet new people and to make friends. Since I had some knowledge and experience in ladies softball, I met people from local teams, tried out for one of the teams and eventually joined them on a full time basis.

I made some new friends who enjoyed trail rides, camping and cross country skiing in the Kananaskis country. Some of these people went skiing every Sunday and invited me to join them. It was good exercise, lots of fresh air, and helped keep me busy.

As per the ad in the paper, I noticed a firm by the name of Argyle Company, had positions open. They were a more established firm with branches in different cities. It was worth checking it out. As I approached the building, I noticed it was huge with many offices, white with blue trimming which I later learned were the company colors.

The office appeared to be filled with a large number of employees. Feeling a bit on the nervous side, I entered the reception room and greeted by friendly receptionist who introduced herself as Jessica. She had long black hair, tall, and appeared attractive with a good personality.

Jessica escorted me to the waiting room near the manager's office and offered me coffee. She said make yourself comfortable as the manager was presently in a meeting.

While I waited for the manager, I checked the surroundings, it appeared to be a friendly place and there was a lot of staff. The manager's office seemed to have nice furniture but the sofa appeared to be out of place. I had heard all kinds of rumors about business offices but I ignored them.

The manager went by the name of Walter (Wally), was approximately 5-7" tall, wore glasses, dark hair and appeared to be the type that liked to play the field. I did not know at the time that his marriage was on the rocks. I waited patiently while the manager and assistant were in a discussion in his office.

After the assistant left, I was ushered into the manager's office and asked to be seated. He offered me coffee we discussed the position available. Joking he said I am only hiring girls that play ball. I must have appeared a bit shocked and felt this guy comes right to the point, no beating around the bush.

Seeing my dismay, he quickly said don't get me wrong and stated they were forming a lady's softball team and needed more players. He was hoping I was a ballplayer and would be willing to join the team. He requested I bring my glove to work as they were planning a practice the next work day. I wasn't sure if he hired me for the job or for the ball team. The team name was "Argyle Angels".

I was interested in playing with his team, but I had to talk to the team I was with now, as I did not want to leave them stranded. I was their main pitcher but I did not tell Wally that I did some pitching at that time or what position I played. He was okay with me dealing with the other team before joining his.

He advised me I was hired and could report for work immediately if I was available. The interview was on Friday and I started work there on Monday. I was advised I would be reporting to Lynn who was the assistant manager at the branch.

She seemed to be a nice girl with blond hair and almost the same age as him. He stated she had just transferred from another province and needed an assistant herself. The position open was to help her. I found she had a nice personality and was easy to get along with. It was the type of position I had in mind.

Jessica, the receptionist had her eye on Wally, but he did not seem to pay any attention to her no matter how hard she tried. Apparently he had his eye on someone else. It did not take long for her to figure it out and she was not happy about it. Hearing this gossip Jessica chose to move to a different environment.

After working for Lynn for some time, I noticed she was very friendly with the manager and they held a lot of private meetings. Since they were both separated from their mates, there appeared to be an attraction between them but everyone was okay with it and minded their own business.

By now the secret was out and all were aware. They lived at the same address and had same employer. However, they always showed the staff respect, appreciation and often gave compliments.

Chapter Five

Wally was also the coach for the team, and the team did well that year but he preferred things be done his way. Some players felt he was just too strict. I was working for him, playing for his team and had no problems with his coaching. He was the only one willing to coach from all the other males in the office.

Most of the girls stuck it out for awhile and those that were unhappy with his coaching slowly weeded out. I gained some experience from the previous teams I played with and tried to help the team achieve their goal and resolve situations.

Wally was pleased that I could play several positions and that I joined their team. I tried to follow the coach's instructions even if I did not agree at times.

I started as a fielder and did not mind. I was happy to have a place on team and the players all showed me respect. At one particular game the team showed up minus the pitcher. The only pitcher on the team was unable to be at the game and with no pitcher the team would have to default.

In the warm ups, I was just fooling around pretending to pitch and did not realize that Wally was watching. Obviously he was trying to see who would fit in for that position. Wally surveyed my throwing for a few minutes, and then he said to me, "you are it". I looked at him dismayed and replied," I am what?"

He stared me right in the eyes and said you will have to pitch today. We do not have a pitcher and you are able to get the ball across the plate. I know you can handle it he said and walked away, he was not aware that I had some pitching experience.

I was a nervous wreck and shivers ran up my spine even before we got started. Although I had some pitching experience I was afraid to let this team down. I decided to give it my best shot no matter what happens.

Our team did not have uniforms but it didn't seem to bother us, our goal was to win. I walked to the mound in my grey sweats, my new runners and I let my pride take over. We had a rivalry with this team and were not going to let them undermine us.

We were not concerned with what the other team was wearing and the team counted on me to help them win the game. Finally the ninth inning rolled in and I was able keep the team on the winning side.

The team and I agreed we had to raise some funds for uniforms so we could look like other teams, but had to make do with what we had for the mean time.

The following week we had to play this team again, only this time we came prepared. We all agreed to wear shorts and matching T-shirts. Some of the players were not comfortable with this type of attire but agreed to go along with the plan. Even the umpires were impressed with our matching attire.

We were the home team and as we dispersed on the field the umpire said in a loud voice....Play Ball.

Charlene was the first batter on the opposing team. She held her bat up high and pretended to crowd the plate. As the first pitch came in, it caught the inside of the plate. Strike one.....yelled the umpire.

On the second pitch, Charlene lost sight of the ball because she was looking elsewhere and did not see the ball go by. The umpire hollered ...Strike Two.

By now the frustration set in and Charlene was terribly upset with the umpire. She rudely yelled to him "Don't you know the strike zone, that was not a strike". He ignored her lack of sportsmanship and said my call stands. The catcher winked at the umpire and smiled.

Often strange things happen in competitive sports or games. Sometimes, people get too competitive, or too emotional, when they participate in these activities. Sports are meant to give you physical exercise and enjoyment. Teamwork plays a big part in both work and play.

If you do not enjoy yourself in the sport you chose, then, you should quit participating and not frustrate yourself. In every sport, there is always a winner and a loser. Both teams usually play well but sometimes one team just puts out that little more effort that counts.

I, also, learned to be competitive as time went on and at times felt disappointment when we lost, but we must accept the outcome no matter what it is.

Back at the ballgame, Charlene was still at the plate, determined to hit my pitches. She remarked, let's see what you can do now. I was annoyed by her remark so I threw the ball as hard as I could. Fortunately it crossed the plate and Charlene missed it as she swung her bat.

Strike three.... yelled the umpire. Charlene appeared stunned and not happy as she walked off the field.

Since a lot of pitchers were inexperienced they often threw a lot of wild pitches and you did not want to get hit by the ball even though we wore helmets.

As it was my turn to bat, I walked up to the plate and I flashed a smile at Charlene who was on the mound. As the umpire said "play ball", Charlene wound up and threw the ball. When the ball came towards me I bunted and the ball landed on the diamond. The runners on base headed for the home plate as I sprinted to first base.

As Charlene leaped to catch the ball, she tripped and lost her balance, safe", yelled the umpire as the players came home. Frustrated, she picked herself up, dusted off and attempted to pitch again.

Our team claimed the win to that game. Here my career as a fastball pitcher began. I spent many years being involved in that sport and enjoyed many good times.

Wally continued to help me with my pitching while I stayed with that company and we remained in the recreational fun league for a number of years. We eventually raised funds for uniforms, jackets and tournament entry fees. We stayed with the team name, "Argyle Angels", as long as the team existed.

Back at the ranch, Wally and Lynn became inseparable and continued their affair in spite of the gossip. Lynn was also on the ball team so it was hard to avoid them. I got along with both, minded my own business.

The staff members indulged in weekly social gatherings at the local pub. Since the staff got a long well, we were like one big family. But after a few cool ones people started talking and sometimes things are said that shouldn't be said creating gossip. I did not indulge much in liquid diets so I often declined going with them. Being on my own at the time, I did not feel like socializing a lot and chose other interests.

I decided to take a few night school courses at the University and enrolled in business accounting and shorthand. Shorthand was used a lot at that time especially by receptionists and secretaries so I thought maybe one day I would use it.

I passed with 70% which was good for me not being able to attend college or university earlier. I also successfully completed an Accounting Development and Training Program with the firm I worked for and passed with a high score.

Chapter Six

Back at the office, Abby was on holidays when I started and I didn't meet her for a couple of weeks. She knew her job well but for some unknown reason not all the girls were friendly towards her. She was attractive, smart dresser, young and divorced. I befriended her, we became good friends and we often helped each other out.

She had a young daughter in kindergarten who was a very good student and very smart for her age. I agreed to babysit her daughter Jody to help her out but sometimes I had to deal with her tantrums. She was spoiled and was never denied anything. I managed to work things out with her and we got along.

Abby lived in a quaint apartment in my neighborhood. She drove a fancy expensive car after receiving a large inheritance. Since we both had an hour for lunch and lived close to the office, we often took lunch together.

Bart, one of the guys in the office, grew fond of Abby. I thought he was happily married but maybe the fire at home was slowly burning out. The three of us started having lunch together at her place or mine. I guess I kind of chaperoned, it was really uncomfortable for me, but I had to go along with the plan so it didn't look suspicious.

The attraction between Bart and Abby grew, and later he and his wife separated. She seemed to be a nice person but didn't mix much with staff so we hardly knew her. They eventually moved in together, but Jody was a handful for Bart. He had no kids of his own and was not experienced in dealing with children.

Since Abby was jealous of Bart, she found it uncomfortable at times in the office so she chose to leave the firm and he transferred to another branch. Eventually they parted ways and Abby left the city. I missed them both as we had lots in common.

While they were dating we did a lot together. She had a brother who owned a farm and sometimes the three of us visited him on weekends. Her brother was divorced and supported a young son who lived with him. He was a gracious host, but we did not have much in common. She visited his farm often as he was her only family here.

The branch I worked at had at least 12-15 employees at most times. This group was close knit, and everyone looked out for each other.

I was made aware they needed employees at a different branch and asked if I would transfer. They informed me that problems occurred at the branch and the executive staff was trying to resolve the issues. Apparently an incumbent and management staff had an issue they could not resolve and the matter resulted in being a legal battle.

When the case was settled, the assistant manager resigned, creating a financial problem for himself due to his stress and left the city for a few months. He left his wife and 3 kids with no means of support. He finally got his act together and made arrangements to pay back his debts. After working things out with his family, they moved on.

The manager of that particular branch was demoted. Shortly after, he left the firm as he was unable to resolve the problems, some of which he created himself. Some of the staff left at the firm's request.

I remained at this branch for some time. Lynn followed me to the branch, and Wally transferred to a different branch. They continued to live together and work for same company.

A new supervisor was transferred to the branch I was at. On the first day Jake showed up in a T-shirt, sports pants, sport shoes and advised the staff he was going golfing as soon as he met the staff. I guess it was his way of making an impression on his staff. Jake was a nice looking guy, married and seemed very friendly. Soon he joined the group on their regular outings while his wife sat at home.

The new manager, Kasper arrived a few weeks later. He created good morale in the office and was well liked by the co-workers. He spent approximately 5-6 months at our branch.

He was then promoted and transferred to the branch where I started. He only stayed a year or so and left the firm. His daughter, Kate joined our firm for a short time but left before he did. She ended up marrying a co-worker, later divorced and moved away.

Within the year of his new posting, Wally took a transfer out of city and Lynn agreed to join him but she would be taking a job with a different firm. They decided to get married before they moved away. Their wedding was small and only close friends and family were invited. I was able to attend this function and we kept in touch for a while.

While I was at this branch, management staff changed many times. Parker joined us as the next manager. He was a stocky fellow, and always told us he was half Ukrainian and half French. He was married and had three children. His wife had previously worked for the same firm in another city. He had a good personality and treated staff well. With him at the reins our office was known as "Best in the West".

For a small office, the executives were pleased with the profits of the branch and we were highly praised. He loved his job and did it well. He was one of the best managers I had worked with at that firm. He was always friendly and available when you needed a helping hand with your assignments. The firm did well at drumming up business and our office did their part to contribute.

The firm held many contests, but with no cash bonuses, instead you had to built up points and then they allowed you to purchase merchandise from their catalogue. We won lots of contests and acquired a lot of valuable items such as lamps, sewing machines and yard furniture. Some of the items, I still have and use on a regular basis.

At this branch I became friends with Elsa. She was unable to have children and decided she would adopt a couple. She originally adopted a girl and then a boy year or so later. Elsa worked part-time after getting her second child when she had babysitting arranged.

Occasionally she brought them to the office and we all enjoyed cuddling them. Her son was a quiet child and never cried much when he was in the office. You could put his chair by your desk and never hear a peep from him unless he wanted his bottle. He always seemed to be a happy camper.

As time went on, there were more changes there during my time at that branch. We had a collector named Carson who had his girlfriend transferred to our branch as they were planning to get married. Unfortunately this did not happen as tragedy struck. Alma was very heart broken.

A couple of weeks before the wedding Carson went boating with his friends. He was not a good swimmer and did not wear a life jacket when the accident took his life. Eventually Alma found another position elsewhere and left us. At the firm, we missed losing both of them as they were well liked and good workers.

The company decided to down size and close some of the smaller branches, and our office was one of them. A couple of workers and I transferred back to the starting branch.

After being 15 years with the firm, Parker left the company and moved to another big city west of us and decided to go into business for himself selling antique furniture. This business did not go well as he was too kind-hearted, and trusted everyone to pay on time and they did not.

Eventually his business could not take any more losses and he became very distressed. Parker left us after going through a depression period but will always be remembered by many that worked with him.

His wife Glena and I became friends, still remain friends and keep in touch. She visited me recently and we had lunch. She raised her daughters on her own and they are doing okay.

Depression not only hurts the person involved but also the people around you.

Chapter Seven

In 1977 I befriended one of the executives named Nigel and his common-law wife. They had purchased an older home here earlier but made plans to move back east and needed to sell their home. Cindy decided to do some minor renovations and paint the place to make it more attractive for sale.

I had become good friends with her and we spent a lot of time together when he was out of town. She enlisted me in helping her with the renovations. We spent many days removing wallpaper of some of the walls that had at least three coats. After the wallpaper was removed we painted the walls and did what else needed to be done.

In return for my help, they offered to fly me to the big city down east where he would be taking on his new position. I spent two glorious weeks in Toronto, Windsor and Niagara Falls and enjoyed every bit of it. We were at the CN Tower when we were given the news that Elvis

Presley had passed on. They also took me to some Blue Jays games.

A year or so later Cindy and Nigel moved to the Vancouver area. Cindy had some minor surgery and something went wrong with the anesthetic. After surgery she became paralyzed from the neck down. She was such a special person and it was heart breaking. Her family moved her back down east where they lived and we lost contact.

After playing softball for a number of years with the Argyle Angels team, which was mostly co-workers, I decided to continue playing softball after the team disbanded. I formed my own team and joined a higher level of ball which they now referred to the game as fastball.

This meant the pitching was faster and you had to train harder to be an accurate pitcher. It also meant you needed proper uniforms and had fees to pay besides buying equipment. We needed a sponsor, so I started shopping around but they were not plentiful.

Several of the ball players including me registered for a mechanics course for women at a small Auto Body Shop. We all passed the course. We learned to change a flat tire, check oils and miscellaneous other important things that needed to be done.

We got to know the owner well, so I approached him to sponsor us. He agreed to help a bit with uniforms and equipment and this made a big difference to us. He wanted his company name in the name of the team so we called our team the "Cosmo Comets".

I did some pitching at first but then I found other players to replace me and I carried on as their coach. I also went to the clinics and became a qualified coach with a Level Two Certificate. Later I recruited assistant coaches to help me because sometimes I had to fill in for missing players.

It was hard to be coach and player in the same game. We entered a few local tournaments and did well at some of them. At one of the tournaments, the last game ended up in a tie. I had to pitch a total of 12 innings in the game. Unfortunately we did not win, as everyone was tired and there were a few errors made.

Upon returning to the branch where I started, I found the firm had made some changes and it was now the largest branch in the city. They had combined their executive office with the branch office as they had lots of space in the building. A hallway separated the executive office and the branch. This meant they had more control as to what was happening at the branch.

The new manager at this branch was Russ. He seemed friendly, helpful and liked by the staff, but things slowly changed. Picking favorites for your team, often results in some unpleasant situations which are hard to control. He also became very good friends with someone I befriended.

The executive realized his actions were creating poor morale at the branch and there was gossip going around, so they created a new position for him in the executive office. However, he remained there for a short period of time only and then chose to move on.

One of the co-workers, Marcy and I became good friends while she was there but it did not last long as she became pregnant with her second child and decided to leave and raise her family. Her husband was employed with the University and had a fairly good income.

Less than a year later, a new manager by the name of Marcus arrived. He was tall and married with 3 children. He liked bowling, so we formed a bowling league at work and it lasted for a while. We enjoyed outings as a group and had a number of social events. He was friendly and showed the staff respect but he also had his bad days. On those days we tried to avoid him.

Often when people experience financial problems, they choose to commit fraud, and sometimes it ruins their careers. I experienced several situations of this sort with this firm.

In one situation, an assistant manager with a large family, experienced financial problems, and was desperate. She felt her only solution was, to create false loans, which created her heartaches instead. In another situation, the manageress tried to cover up gambling debts for her boyfriend with fraud loans. However, these people were able to work out amicable arrangements to pay the funds back.

I believe this people learned their lesson the hard way. Eventually they both were able to obtain new positions and move on with life.

In the early part of '78, I decided to go on a trip to Disneyworld with my niece also (godchild). We toured Disneyworld as much as we could while we were there. I was at Disneyland previously but there are always new things to see.

We took in places such as Adventure land, Tom Sawyer's Island, Fantasy Land, and took rides on the boats and Monorail. We took a number of pictures with the mascots. Mickey and Minnie were favorites for everyone. Even adults can have fun at both places.

Later, my niece moved in with me and found work in the city. Then another niece joined us and they got their own apartment. Eventually she decided to take up nursing and still works occasionally. She married later, and they have two daughters and a granddaughter.

We had one problem on the trip after we left Toronto. While we were in the air for a short time, they discovered a problem with the landing gear. We returned to the airport and boarded a different plane. It did scare a few passengers but all went well and we arrived at our destination safely.

In the latter part of the same year, my younger brother, who was in Williams Lake, was now living in Estevan, Sask. He had accepted a job with a Community Pasture Ranch. He loved his job riding horses and herding cattle and wasn't ready to change his career at this time.

A number of our family members, including my older brother, his wife and two children, my younger sister and her two children and I decided to visit him at this ranch. We travelled in 2 vehicles, too many for one. Since it was a long trip we camped one day going there and one day back.

My brother and his wife lived in a small ranch house on the acreage. There were lots of turtles in that area. The huge turtles swam in the small pools of water and sloughs near his yard. They ended up sunning on his front yard. The younger crowd really enjoyed them and it was like having a zoo. The turtles were not afraid of people and we were able to pet them.

Upon returning to work, I found Bart had been transferred back to this branch. Some new co-workers, Gene and Fran transferred in due to their branch closing. Tess was hired as a receptionist so we had a lot of new faces.

After a few months Gene starting dating Tess and Bart became interested in Fran. Before I left the firm, Bart and Gene married their mates. Gene moved to another city and Bart joined a financial firm in a nearby community.

Several of the other co-workers I befriended soon moved on too. Gina who was single transferred to the Lethbridge branch and later to a different branch. She married and raised two sons. She worked for a short time with Wally at his branch.

After Gina left, Delia decided to join our firm. She was Ukrainian and we had lots in common. She was a single mom and we had some good times together. After a short stint she chose the banking field and stayed there until retirement. She did sell her condo and lived in my area for some time.

One of the co-workers, Tom had left our firm and went into the banking system and seemed to enjoy it. It was basically the same line of work with more pay and more chances for advancement. Another co-worker from our firm joined him.

After being with his new firm just over a year he tried to convince me to make a change also. He advised me there were a couple positions open with the firm in his department. I had been with the present firm over 6 years, raises were limited and not many chances for advancement and maybe it was time to move on.

I discussed the position with Tom and advised him I would consider making a change but I needed to know more about the firm and the position. Tom advised me of the benefits and the possibility of advancing. He made his supervisor aware of my experience and that I may be interested in the position.

His supervisor was happy to hear about a prospect for the position and advised Norton at the Human Resources Department. Norton called me several times to arrange for interviews. He was pleasant, very convincing, had a good personality and even bought me lunch on several occasions. He advised there would be advancements, better pay and benefits.

I wasn't fully convinced that this was the right job for me at the time and did not want to give up a place and position I liked. Also I wanted to learn more about the firm before making a decision.

I had already agreed to go out of town for the Argyle Company as they decided to close the branch in Brooks. It was a smaller community and business was not doing so well. I advised Norton I would make my decision upon my return.

Norton was anxious to hire someone soon and apparently wanted me to join their firm. He kept calling me in Brooks pressuring me to make a decision. Finally, he offered me a little more money than previously. It was a whole $50.00 and in those days $50.00 was a lot of money when you did not have much.

I was prepared to look at new challenges and advised Norton I was looking for advancement which would produce more pay, and would discuss negotiations at a later date.

While I was away, Norton had lined up a position for me and hoped I would accept his offer. I agreed to accept the position and resigned after Norton informed what the position would be and the benefits that came with it.

I had participated in a saving plan with my previous employer for over 6+ years. The firm matched the amount in savings and I came out with a fair amount of funds.

I had managed to save enough to purchase my first home. I invested in a duplex and luckily I had a good neighbor on the other side. We got a long well and there were no problems.

I stayed in this duplex until 1988. Then purchased a bigger home with a double garage and a big backyard.

Chapter Eight

It was a warm and sunny day in October, 1979 when I joined Norton's company, which was the Milton Banking Corporation, and I was hired as a loans and collection officer with a fair amount of responsibility. I was happy to have the opportunity to challenge this position.

Norton later informed me he was sending me to a different branch which was located across town from me and transportation was limited to the area at that time. It meant that I would have to invest into a vehicle to get to work on time and incur expenses. This situation was discussed with Norton and he said he would look into the matter.

The first position offered was in the main downtown area where transportation was more accessible. Norton insisted that I take the second position and offered me an extra $50.00 in salary to cover my travel expenses. It wasn't a big amount but it helped with gas expenses.

These days it is change for the parking meter. I ended up starting at the Union branch.

He informed me the company had many affiliate branches and if I felt I did not want to stay at that facility I could transfer at a later date. I went shopping and purchased a lime green pinto. This vehicle was in my price range and took me from point A to point B.

The fluorescent green stood out like a sore thumb but it was easy to find when it got dark. I was living in a small duplex at the time and parked the car in the back of the duplex. After parking the car one evening someone was gutsy enough to steal the cheap radio out of the car. This person must have really been broke because the radio was not worth much.

The office was located in a small shopping mall and wasn't a very big branch but seemed to have lots of staff. When I arrived at that office for my first day of work I was greeted by Harvey who introduced himself as the manager of that department.

I surveyed the surroundings and detected that this was one crowded office. He took me over and introduced me to my desk. The other desks were so close together we could almost play footsy. Each time you left your desk you were accidently bumping into either the desks or other people.

I was given a small desk, three desks from the supervisor, but I did not mind. Privacy was very limited and at some desks it did not exist. Everyone tried to accommodate each other without getting upset and tried not to disrupt anyone. They appeared to be a close knit group and I hoped I would be accepted to their team and I was.

Harvey was a great supervisor with a great personality. He was pleasant, helpful, and had an excellent attitude. His sense of humor kept the team working together. He always joked with his staff and said he had a rule for new employees.

The rule was you have to buy in and when you leave you have to buy out. The staff did occasionally socialize and we always had good times.

Harvey was in his mid-thirties, stocky person and enjoyed life to the fullest. He never presented himself as "the person in charge" but always as being part of the group.

Good teamwork produced good business and kept executives happy. He was certainly right for this job and the staff had lots of respect for him just like he did for the staff. He never criticized, only encouraged people to do better which would benefit them not him.

I worked hard to achieve the figures desired by management and communicated well with the co-workers. The firm only wanted people who understood the clients' circumstances and showed them some compassion when dealing with them.

With the experience I gained previously, I was able to assist a lot of the clientele and help them make the best of things. I was impressed with the talented staff they had. The manager was happy, the staff showed each other respect, and all went well.

At that time we were expected to make house calls to clientele who experienced financial problems and were unable to keep their commitments. These were day time calls, and we usually went in pairs to any particular residence. I also made several calls on my own as required.

On one particular day a male co-worker and I went on a field call to a residence where the debtors refused co-operate and would not answer their phone or respond to letters sent. They let us in the house but became very upset when we asked for payment. The male debtor picked up a small item and threw it towards the door where my co-worker was standing and asked us to leave. Fortunately it only hit the door.

After this episode, the firm determined it would not be in the best interest to send females out on field calls. The manager became concerned and hired special agents to do field calls and misc duties. A lot of low income families lived in the area, with little or no income and some only received some type of government assistance. In spite of the circumstances, we tried to show patience and be understanding to all clientele.

I continually tried hard to achieve the goals expected of me. Harvey was greatly impressed when I achieved them and so was Norton. It was a good atmosphere to work in and we found it easier to achieve goals because the good teamwork. I felt I might be on the road to success. It was nice for this country bumpkin to be appreciated and not criticized.

At this time I had no computer experience, but I befriended several girls at the branch who helped me with banking and on other situations. They were true friends and I could count on them to bail me out if necessary.

After spending some time at this branch, I decided to trade my car in and buy a more reliable one so I could do some travelling. I bought a new blue mustang. My nephew moved to Vancouver to play hockey and attend school there. He had a one bedroom apartment and said

I could always bunk on the couch. He was with the New West minister Bruins at the time, a junior team.

I booked my holidays during the summer and kept myself busy while he was at school. I had made several trips to Vancouver using the map he made for me so I had the trip down pat. I always travelled during the day and never got lost getting to his place. In those days I guess I was not afraid to travel alone. I often brought back fruit from BC for myself and others.

One of my brother-in-laws, a trucker suggested I carry a radio in case I run into problems. He set up the radio for me and my code was "Mustang Sally". When I got bored, I talked to the 18 wheelers. Soon I had more than enough callers so I gave up the radio.

On one trip I took a friend who had befriended some people before they moved to Victoria. They had extended an invitation to visit them when in the area but I don't think they really expected her to show up. We got up early the next day after we arrived and took the ferry to see them.

When we arrived in Victoria we called them. They invited us to their house, but it was very uncomfortable as they didn't seem too excited to see us. We stayed one night only and headed for Qualicum Beach. We spent some time at the beach then headed back to Vancouver.

After spending less than a year at the branch, Norton advised me one day he had received excellent reports about my work, he graciously complimented me on a job well done and told me I was an asset to the firm. He showed me a lot of respect.

He came over to the branch the following day and without hesitation said he had good news for me. He offered me a promotion to another branch with a small increase in salary. He advised the branch needed help with that department and he felt I could assist. I was pleased to hear this and agreed to accept the position.

He advised the staff as to what was happening, and I received many congratulations from the staff. A couple days later we all met in the staff room and the staff showed their gratitude by presenting me with an expensive watch on a chain.

I was so impressed to receive this gift it brought tears to my eyes. I had admired one of the watches a co-worker was wearing and, let her know how much I liked it. I did not expect them to buy me one. Before I left I was obligated to buy out of the department.

This firm held many social events usually once a month for all the staff to attend with a small entrance fee as they supplied a meal. Before moving on to the new branch, I attended a social gathering at a local restaurant. At each gathering they either had a speaker or some other entertainment.

This particular time they decided to have a fashion show with the executive modeling ladies' outfits. Some of the outfits were very impressive. Norton dressed as a cleaning lady. He walked around the tables with a dust mop.

As he walked around dusting tables he accidently on purpose spilled the vice president's beer on his new suit. The vice president, was not impressed as he did not dress up for the occasion.

The best dressed person was Dudley. He chose to dress as one of the "ladies of the night". He was hilarious and tried to preposition the executives all night telling them he was a high priced call girl. Dudley and I became good friends while we both worked for the firm. He invited many to dance with him but some declined.

Usually at these events liquor is involved and sometimes liquor talks. That night I heard a lot of bragging about things which were best untold because they only started gossip.

Dudley held several positions over a period of time before leaving. We remained friends while he was with the firm. Over a period of times there were many staff changes at all the branches. Staff seemed to move from branch to branch on a regular basis.

Chapter Nine

I transferred to the Tartan Branch which was smaller and had fewer staff. My first impression was this office was not as warm and not as welcoming as the one I left. The atmosphere appeared different. As I entered the branch I introduced myself to the receptionist who was polite and appeared friendly.

She took me to the manager's office and introduced me to Norma. She seemed friendly enough and being a family person with several grown children she seemed okay. Her position was new and like everyone else there she had lots to learn and lots of responsibility. She seemed to show respect for staff and didn't seem to show favoritism which was a bonus to this office.

The move to this office was instigated by Norton because of my previous performance and I hoped things would go good here. I was happy to have the extra pay as I was travelling out of town a lot because of family. Our mother had a stroke and had to be placed in a nursing home as she needed constant care. She actually had more than one stroke before she left us.

Due to the circumstances, I wanted to visit our mom as much as possible. My car was getting old by that time but I could not afford another one on my pay. I didn't have any serious problems with the car at that time so I continued making the trips mostly on long weekends and holidays.

At this branch I became a junior supervisor, but I also remained as a loan and collection officer. I felt it was a great opportunity to advance and had two other co-workers assisting me. There was some pressure but I handled it to the best of my ability.

My desk was by the window and in front of the vault. We were shown how to get out of the vault often, just in case something happened. I always worried that if there was a robbery I'd be the first one they would pick on. Fortunately this never happened.

While working at this office I continued to try and keep my ball team together, as the cost of living was going up and so was the cost of sports. My previous sponsor advised me he was closing his business and could no longer sponsor our team. It wasn't easy to get a sponsor, but I had befriended some clients at this office and asked if they knew anyone that would help. I had contacted many firms but they declined.

A few days later one of clients I had solicited for sponsorship contacted me and advised they could not sponsor my team but maybe their head office would. He said the owner sponsored other sports down east where the head office was. They were only a small office here and were unable to offer financial backing. He suggested I contact the owner so I did. I explained to him about my team and he agreed to help out.

They did not have many stipulations, only that they wanted the players to wear their company hats to advertise their firm. He requested a group picture of the team each year. I told him this would not be a problem, and the deal was sealed. He advised me the funds would be in the mail within a few days.

As promised, I received the funds within three days. I could not believe how graciously they agreed to accommodate my team. The funds not only bought us new uniforms, paid for new equipment but gave us a little extra.

We also used their company name on our uniforms and now became the "ABSO Raiders." I recruited some new players and one of the player's husband agreed to coach, and I remained as manager and player.

Back at the branch we had some good times too. The whole staff dressed up at Halloween and the customers loved it. I befriended one of the girls who had red hair and she liked to be called "Red" as her nickname. She insisted that she was going to dress like a little red devil and did. She was a barrel of laughs at social events and always fun to be with. Even though she was slightly handicapped, she moved around good with her walking problem.

I dressed as the "Pink Panther" as it was popular at that time. Some staff dressed as jailbirds, the manager, Norma as a policewoman, and others as clowns. Fun was had by all that day and we celebrated after work at the local pub with our costumes on.

Christmas was also an enjoyable time at the branch. Each year we exchanged fun gifts with the other staff members. We bought items that we could later donate to charities that really needed gifts for the less unfortunate people and always put in a little extra.

I had received good training from Harvey and put it to use. All seemed to go well in this office, until we had a new supervisor transferred to the branch. She came from the auditing department, and appeared to be friendly at first.

Soon we found out she had her own motives and seemed to thrive on gossip. On occasions she attempted to humiliate co-workers in front of other people and later tried to apologize in private. I had to often defend myself as she had favorites.

Wilma was married but did not use her husband's name. I was unable to control a situation, that occurred due to not being informed of the full details. It was her responsibility to make the staff aware of the circumstances.

She chose to embarrass me in front of the co-workers and made me feel very uncomfortable. With the little respect shown, I wondered if taking the move was the right choice.

She loved to play the video machines across the street from us and spent many breaks and lunch hours there. Sometimes she pressured me to go with her but often I declined.

I had worked a whole year at the branch without taking one sick day or special days off. Even though we were allowed ten sick days, I never took any because I was healthy and did not need them. While the audit was being done the inspectors were amazed. They said this did not seem possible that I did not take any sick days.

At the time I was complemented on the perfect attendance. This was short lived because there was no give and take. I even came to work with a sprained ankle. When I asked for a few days off after the audit, because of my sore ankle the management flatly said no, but if I had phoned in sick there would have been no problem.

Since our mom was ill and in a nursing home 300 miles away, I had no choice but to travel if I wanted to visit her. One weekend in December while visiting our mom, my car broke down. I could not get back in time for work. Being the honest person I am, I called the manager and advised her of the circumstances.

I felt they would be sympathetic but they weren't. They said they were not prepared to give me any days off regardless of the circumstances. I explained my car was not safe to drive as small flames were coming out from under the hood of the car .The mechanic said it would take at least two days to fix the problem. I had no choice but to stay till the car was fixed.

I discussed it with Norma and she advised me I would be docked for the days of work I missed and could not use sick days for this. I completed 10 extra days of work for them and they were not prepared to negotiate. Upon my return both Norma and Wilma said they were following company policy.

After several discussions I was advised if I had phoned in sick there would not have been any issues. I was disappointed in their response. If I wanted to be dishonest I could have easily had the family doctor there give me a form saying I was sick but I wasn't that type.

Several days later I was advised that the firm will not dock my pay but rather will take two days off my vacation. Either way being honest I was doomed. I wasn't ready to give up so I contacted the Human Resources office. All the people I spoke to had the same attitude. They wasted more valuable hours trying to decline my request than the two days off were worth.

Finally I spoke to Norton who hired me. He was still with the executive office and he advised me to phone in sick for two days. I conveniently got sick on my holidays and collected the 2 days before I returned to work. I made sure I collected the ten days each year going ahead.

Another co-worker experienced a similar problem. Her young daughter got violently ill overnight and she did not want to leave her with a babysitter. She called the branch and told the manager the truth. She was advised that if she did not show up for work they would dock a day's pay. If she had phoned in and said she was sick, there would have been no problem and that disappointed her.

One of the girls I befriended decided we should go on a vacation. She had never been to Las Vegas and wanted me to go with her. We took in the sights of Las Vegas and had a great time. We did not win much but at the same time did not spend much. April was fun to be with and we spent a lot of time together until she befriended a client.

The love between them blossomed and you know the rest of the story. They got married, started their own family, and she decided to stay at home and raise her family. She had been doing extremely well and had a number of promotions but her family was more important.

While working at this branch, I often covered for other employees at a different branch. The Carson branch was huge and operated on two floors of the building. The downstairs was the actual banking services and upstairs the loan and collection department. While filling in for a co-worker I checked out the credit applications for the car financing department, confirmed insurance and did other miscellaneous duties because of my experience.

After one of my annual reviews, which was completed by the Regional Office staff, they gave me a very good rating. It got to the point where the branch was doing well in our department and collections were certainly under control to their satisfaction. I was happy with my position and was not considering any changes at this time.

One day a junior executive showed up at our office and said he needed to talk to me. He was small built and not very tall and didn't seem to show much respect for others. He told me to join them in a meeting in the manager's office and I complied.

During the meeting he stated there was a position they needed to fill and were looking for someone with my experience. He further stated I had no choice but to accept his offer. Karl never explained the position nor did he offer incentive or anything else. He must have felt his job was done.

I felt that this conversation was not handled professionally and his attitude was somewhat different. I did not know how to react to his comments. I had never encountered such behavior previously. I was pressured to take a position without reviewing the pros and cons.

I was not sure what his reaction would be if I had declined. Norma sat by and did not interfere perhaps she was afraid to say anything at the time. All she said "you completed the duties here well and you will do well there". I tried several times but did not get the opportunity to discuss the position.

From 1979 to 84, I held several positions and enjoyed working both sides of the fence, now he pushing me to transfer to the collection department. I wasn't prepared to make a quick decision so I contacted Head office and arranged a meeting, expecting some respect and sympathy.

I might have been more reluctant to accept the position, had it been presented in a different manner and without so much pressure, but it was demanded I take the position. I had numerous discussions with different executives before it was suggested I try the position for 3 months. They further stated that after 3 months I could stay there or arrange for a transfer. It was a lateral move.

I was also advised that Karl was married to Tina whom I worked with at the previous branch. I did not know her well and had never met her husband only their young son. She loved to entertain and often invited staff members to her home, and I was fortunate to attend some of the events.

Tina held baby showers, wedding showers and other social events at her home and was proud to do it. Karl was never there when we visited their home and she claimed he was always working late. At that point I didn't know any different.

I was informed that at the new branch, the supervisor was recently promoted to a junior supervisor and had limited experience in that position. I had no idea there was more to it. Even though I did not appreciate as the way this the matter was handled, I made the decision to try this position for 3 months and then determine if I wanted to stay on at that branch.

Chapter Ten

It is now 1984, and I was assigned a new position as an administrative assistant. My duties were to focus on collection portfolio of overdue, visa, bad debt and skip tracing accounts. I was also expected to provide prompt courteous customer service to all the clients, listen carefully to their individual needs and deliver the best level of service in a friendly manner. I was to attend small claims court and bankrupt offices as required.

The office was located downtown, and parking was at a premium but I was lucky to find parking 4 blocks away as long as I got there fairly early in the morning. The public transportation for that area was not the best at the time and it was hard to hitch a ride with someone else on a regular basis. This location was known as the Hilton branch.

As I arrived at the office, I was greeted by a female who introduced herself as Nita. She was a bit taller than me, black hair and in the age bracket of 20-30. She seemed pleasant but acted strangely. I sensed there was something going on that I was not aware of.

The greeting and first meeting was unbelievable. She did not make me feel welcome, from the moment I entered the office, and the office appeared to have a cold atmosphere.

She advised me in a manner which was unacceptable, that she heard I was not happy about taking the position and that I felt I was forced to take it. I tried to give her my side of the situation but she immediately responded I am not interested in your sad story. Wow, it was like a slap in the face. This happened even before I started work there.

I just could not understand why I got the cold shoulder and why she reacted that way. I was there for her benefit not mine, she needed a collector and I was experienced. She wasted little time informing me of her relationship with Karl. She advised they attended the same meetings. She was attracted to him and was looking to a future with him.

She hardly knew me and I hardly knew her but she discussed more about herself than the actual position I was assuming. However, I was already aware of my duties as I was given a job description.

As we walked to the corner, she showed me where my desk was. There were four desks cramped in a small corner for the collectors. The desks were so close to each other that if one person had to leave all had to get up and let the person by. In this cozy corner were Jonas, Greta, Herman and me.

Greta had some experience and a good personality, Herman came from another financial firm, and Jonas had just retired from a government job and was biding his time until he was ready to retire. He decided to try his hand at collections.

Jonas was married and had two daughters. I was befriended by Jonas and his family and welcomed at their home. I often had coffee with his spouse as I lived in the area and we did other socializing.

Nita had her ups and downs. Some days she complemented you for a job well done, other days she found faults. She seemed to be backlogged all the time and decided to recruit Greta as her assistant.

Greta was the same level as us and found it hard to be part time collector and part time supervisor in a position in which she had no experience. After becoming a part time supervisor, she became frustrated from the pressures instilled by Nita and problems arose among the co-workers.

She tried to work both sides of the fence but on many occasions it only created poor morale among the co-workers. She claimed she was following instructions and was trying to please Nita. However, this did not stop the co-workers from getting upset with her.

She also had her own problems, as her common-law husband had medical problems, and was required to take medication daily. If the instructions were not followed, he often experienced reactions and sometimes had to be rushed to the hospital. This only compounded her other problems.

Several months later the auditors came in and sensed tension during their visit. They spent several days observing the goings on and then decided to interview each person in that department separately.

They felt there was a serious morale problem and it had to be dealt with.

When they interviewed her, Greta admitted that she was following instructions but was inexperienced to deal with the situations that incurred on a regular basis. She advised she did not want to work two positions and preferred to return as collector. However the auditors had already determined this just by observing.

The auditors advised the manager of the branch that the attitudes and the morale in the office had to change as it was not acceptable. They further stated this office only needed one supervisor for our department.

This did not sit well with Nita as she had no one to handle her backlogs but Karl convinced her not be so hard on the co-workers. A few weeks down the road, her friendly manner turned to coolness and we were back to square one.

From then on the co-workers chose to voice their opinions when it was necessary. I decided I would stand up for my rights even it meant retaliation later. I always tried to keep a smile on my face but it wasn't always easy and my stubborn pride kept me in this job.

Occasionally, we got together for fish fry dinners as a group. We always met at Nita's house and of course Karl was always there. She eventually mellowed a bit as her love affair with Karl blossomed. Tina met someone else and moved away taking her son with her.

Several months later, Greta asked for a transfer out of the office and the city. They loved water and house boats. They moved to the neighboring province which had lots of lakes.

In this branch we also had two people who made outside calls for collections and many other duties. Larry had been around in this line of work for a number of years, but Tony was previously in the forces. I had received a lot of help from Larry and both treated me with respect.

Larry and Tony both did field trips outside the office, attended court, repossessed vehicles and had miscellaneous duties. Larry left the firm after retiring and we are still in touch. Tony left due to his spouse having an illness and I lost contact with him.

Another part of our office was managed by Andy. He had a different sense of humor and sometimes we did not know how to take his comments. He was originally from the east, but wanted to experience the west. He was close to his family and missed not having them closer to him. His position required him to handle collections also.

His wardrobe wasn't exactly business attire but he was comfortable with it. Eventually he made some changes and it impressed us. He did fraternize with a co-worker from another branch and they shared accommodations as time went on.

He had always longed to head back east so the executive decided to play a joke on him on the first day of April, they advised the manager as to when they would be making the call. When the phone rang, the call was placed on the speaker phone. When they said April fools, no transfer, he was very disappointed, upset and did not appreciate the joke.

Since he was interviewed three times about the transfer he assumed it was real and told his family.

Shortly after he asked for a transfer, when one was arranged he left and we lost contact with him.

While at the branch he had a difference with one of his clientele who owed several thousand dollars. She resented the way she was treated. She contacted different banks, collected $1.00 bills, crumpled them up in a brief case and presented it to him at closing time. I was one of the staff who stayed behind to count the funds and I did not forgive him.

In this branch, our lunch room was down stairs. People always carried coffee upstairs daily. One day someone spilled coffee on the stairs and did not clean it up. I did not notice it when I was walking downstairs, slipped and went flying down the stairs. They made a report up and put it on file that I hurt my knee for future reference. I also put a copy in my personal file in my desk.

One day when I started having problems with my knee and felt I may have to go on short term disability, the report Nita made up mysteriously disappeared. It appeared also someone searched through my personal file and removed my copy too. I just did not understand why this happened. I made sure in the future important documents were kept in a safe place.

Our office was a separate department but since we shared rent with the main branch, a suggestion was made that a joint social fund be established for both departments via payroll deduction.

Everyone had contributed over $100.00 during the time there. When it was time for our office to move we found the fund went dry.

Everyone was upset that there were no funds available. We found out later, the other part of the office used the funds for social gatherings after work and not everyone was always invited. It was very disappointing to hear this happened.

Before we moved to the new location I had already put in five years with this firm and at 5 years you were given an award. Nita was in charge of handling the awards to her employees.

One day Nita said to me; I left your award on your desk. No speech of any kind, and no thanks for a job well done. She just did not seem interested in my accomplishments and did not handle this in a professional manner.

She claimed she constantly had migraine headaches because she was allergic to chocolate but it appeared there was more to it.

Chapter Eleven

In the spring of 1985, the lease at that location was not renewed because the rent went sky high and the firm was not prepared to pay it, they decided we had to move. They located a place for our office and later in the year we moved to the Palmer branch.

The second floor of this branch was converted to an office setting with private entrances. The downstairs of the branch handled the personal banking department, mortgages and the loans. I befriended several of the staff downstairs and became good friends with them. Becky handled the mortgage portfolio and dealt with real estate accounts. She was married and her spouse had his own business.

Allison did receptionist/secretarial work. Her spouse was employed at Regional office. After a stint there Allison was offered a new position, she declined it and left the firm while her spouse stayed on until retirement.

The three of us vowed to stay friends and occasionally we had coffee and gap sessions.

After retirement, Becky and her husband chose to be snowbirds and live in the States part of the time, while Allison and her husband moved to a small community outside the city and do some volunteer work.

Transferring from the old location was Nita, Jonas, Larry, Tony and me. Nita had a fairly big desk and insisted it had to go to the new location. Her desk took up half the office space and the rest of us shared the other half. After being there a short time, we were advised more staff would be added.

With the big desk we found the office was crowded and even with many windows we had little light. They placed dividers to give the collectors more privacy and the only one getting the most light was the desk. Since we required more room the big desk had to go and this upset Nita as she did not want to part with it.

In the renovations they made room to accommodate 12 employees, making access through two entrances. The customers had their own entrance when they wanted to discuss their accounts.

The receptionist had a small office barely enough to accommodate a small desk and typewriter. The glass around the office was bullet proof because she handled funds and sometimes large amounts. However, we always felt the hole in the middle of the window was too large with room to put a hand through.

We had a couple of really small interview rooms, even though the building was smoke free, we still needed the air to circulate but it didn't. Some of the co-workers had colds constantly so they invested into a humidifier but this machine soon died from exhaustion. My desk was facing cabinets, so I did not have much of a view.

While the renovations were being completed, the employees there prepared a time capsule, with each putting in a personal item and placed it in one of the walls. It remained in the wall for five years.

At this point, I was still involved in sports and decided to continue as a lot of the players were still interested and I did have a sponsor. A lot of teams didn't and found it hard to raise funds but I wasn't ready to give up.

I recruited a good pitcher and her husband agreed to take over the coaching and I remained as manager and player. He coached our team for several years and all went well. Then he decided that he wanted to move up to higher level of ball and took some of the players with him. His wife was a good pitcher, and he did not want her to give it up but rather make a career of it.

Even though she was a good ball player and loved the sport she also wanted a family. When he found out she was pregnant, he was not happy and he pushed her to play while she was pregnant. She decided to take time off for the baby to be born and that is when he chose to separate and go his own way.

She quit his team and returned to my team for a short stint. She met someone else who appreciated a family and welcomed her into his life. He agreed to raise her son and eventually she dissolved her previous marriage. Her ex carried on with his team and had his own affairs.

At this point I was back to coaching alone again, some of the husbands and boyfriends tried to help out but conflicts occurred so I ended up being coach, manager and player. Then we went to a local tournament and I met several people and the umpires. I befriended an umpire and discussed the coaching with him. Chuck said he was interested in helping to coach the team.

He had coached teams before and had the experience. We became friends and we started dating. Eventually I convinced him to help coach and we carried the team for several years as I still had the sponsor who was assisting me graciously and a lot of our expenses were paid.

We also raised funds and charged a player fee to help with out of town tournaments. We enjoyed the sport, met a lot of people and entered many tournaments. Managing and coaching a team helped relieve some of the pressures at work. It gave me something to think about other than work.

Besides being an umpire, he was also a referee and went to many tournaments out of town. While attending a tournament in Victoria, I agreed to meet him in Vancouver and travel home together. I hadn't travelled by train previously so that year I chose to take the train from our city to Vancouver. My nephew's wife picked me up and I stayed with them until we left for home.

Meanwhile back the ranch in 1986, after the renovations were completed, staff changes were made. Nita transferred to another position. They brought Tyler in to replace Nita. He had a great personality, good attitude and married with two sons. He was easy to get along with and treated the staff well. He always believed in hearing both sides of the story and being fair.

The staff then increased to 12 people including the manager. The management staff was supplied with computers and the rest of us handled things manually. At this point they began recruiting the extra staff required.

Alvin was transferred in from another branch and became a supervisor under the management of Tyler.

He was married but had no family. Both Alvin and his wife were very career minded and their goal was to keep going up. He constantly researched other positions available as he was only interested in advancement.

He had a strange sense of humor and picked on co-workers that he could easily upset as he seemed to get enjoyment out of this. He often made people around him feel very uncomfortable as his jokes were not funny most of the time. Many times his comments were in bad taste. He seemed to target me a lot as he knew I did not appreciate his joking.

I tried to discuss these situations with him but he did not care. I filed several complaints with Tyler, but Alvin always seemed to wiggle his way out, and made it look like he did nothing wrong. He was disciplined by Tyler but it didn't stop him from doing things when Tyler was not around.

By now I had already spent 10 years with this firm and was still going strong. I was determined to make things work. Each five years this firm presented the employees with awards. This was the year I was due for my 10 year award and it was supposed to be presented by Alvin.

After a weekly staff meeting, Alvin stood up and snidely said I have a parcel with your name, I guess it must be for you. It would have been more appropriate for him to at least state, glad to have you aboard or nice job, but like Nita he said absolutely nothing. I was really disappointed in his attitude, especially when he was constantly trying to get promotions.

They also brought in two other employees from other branches, Louis was tall and slim. He was married with two children and had been with the firm for a few years. Fanny was single and did not appear to be dating anyone that we were aware of.

Alvin's attitude did not change and he kept looking for a transfer until he eventually found what he wanted and left. His position was filled with Martha, who was tall, slim and wore expensive clothing. I probably spent the same amount for two or three outfits as she did for one. After all, I was just a farmer's daughter living in a rich man's world.

At first she seemed very pleasant, knowledgeable and appeared to be an asset to the branch, an improvement from Alvin. It appeared she was happily married and seemed to show respect and appreciation. We were not aware there was anything wrong. At that point she did not appear to have favorites and seemed to treat everyone the same.

At this time, I was handling the collection portfolio which consisted of a variety of different accounts the office handled. I did skip tracing and dealt with outside agencies that assisted with some accounts. I attended court cases and bankrupt meetings on a regular basis and always got good reviews on my work.

At the end of this year, Martha began completing my reviews and I expected her to continue with giving me good reviews. But I was wrong as she had other motives.

After completing the annual review she advised she needed to discuss something with me. She did not write up a bad review but stated she had good news for me. At first I was anxious to hear what she had to say but soon I became very disappointed with the outcome.

While discussing the review she stated she found me a new job at another branch and wanted me to take it. I advised her I was not looking for a new position and was happy here for the present time. She said again; "I want you to take this position". I inquired if there was a promotion or raise, there was neither just a lateral move which I was not interested in.

I explained to her that I lived close to the present branch, did not want to face daily traffic jams going to work and saw no reason to move. I would have had to get up at 5 am to make it to work on time and I would be incurring extra expenses for gas, oil, and maintenance of my car plus insurance. With no extra income it was not feasible for me to move.

I soon got the impression she no longer wanted me at the branch. Her face turned red, and in a loud voice, she continued to speak to me in a rude manner. She appeared spiteful and was no longer the pleasant person I met previously. It puzzled me why she acted that way as she gave me good reviews and I did nothing to offend her.

I was not sure why this was happening or how to fix it and she wasn't prepared to discuss the situation. She stated that if I chose not to accept the job, she would make sure I didn't receive any promotions or raises as long as I was there.

I was hoping she didn't really mean this, and eventually this situation would fade away but it didn't. She continued to make my life miserable. I soon realized I had a battle on my hands and I didn't start the war. Strangely enough, she did not treat the rest of the co-workers that way. Obviously, she wasn't aware of the saying "do unto to others as you wish to be done unto you".

I discussed the matter with Tyler, the manager. He tried to smooth things over but she was hard to please. He felt she was on a power trip and tried to convince her to reduce the pressure and for a short period she did. He was not happy with the situations in the office and decided to move on and take another position. He was greatly missed by the co-workers.

The executives chose Martha to assume the management position. Louis was given the position of assistant supervisor, but did not have the experience or attitude for this position. Fanny was promoted to junior supervisor. They were previously the same level as us.

Both had no experience as supervisors, and could have done well, except after getting titles, their attitudes changed drastically and perhaps felt they no longer needed to show respect and appreciation to those who deserved it.

When Fanny was the same level as us, she was easier to get along with and helpful at times when needed. Now she only appeared to be friendly with management and co-workers were afraid to talk to her at times.

She desperately wanted to become Martha's favorite person and complained constantly to her with any rumors she heard whether they were true or not. On occasion she deliberately upset me or other co-workers, or created problems that would upset the co-workers. In her mind she felt this was what Martha wanted.

At weekly staff meetings she always tried to defend us and said; I have your back. Later she would do the reverse and find something to complain about. Eventually the morale in the office changed and others found it hard to trust her.

Jonas got along well with Fanny and she did not hassle him. Often Jonas advised me I could confide in him and occasionally I did. He promised to keep the conversations confidential, but when pressured by Martha, he always gave in. I did not feel confident in discussing some issues,and only discussed ones pertaining to work. When he was away, I covered his desk, as he attended many comrade funerals, curling and golf tournaments.

In 1986, we decided to attend the Expo in Vancouver with my sister and her husband joining us. We travelled by car and stayed with my nephew and his family. It was with their son who played hockey. It was the first time I experienced seeing shows in 3D. I found the Expo very interesting.

After returning to work, I was informed that other co-workers experienced unfair treatment and contacted the executive office. They were unable to achieve satisfaction and felt filing complaints with Human Resources brought no results. They chose to find other positions and left the firm. As a result, the firm lost some dedicated employees because the situations were not handled properly.

Martha continued to pressure me and it caused me to be stressed out. She refused to discuss the problem and suggested I see a doctor or look for new employment if I couldn't handle the stress in this office. She did not seem to care where the stress was coming from.

I had to agree at this point she appeared to be on a power trip as she was in charge of this branch at present. She failed to realize that it was the teamwork that made her look good in her position.

Louis was easier to get along with when Martha wasn't around. His attitude changed when she was there, it looked like he may have been afraid of her. He was great at finding fault with everyone except himself. The whole management personnel seemed to lack understanding, and were unable to show compassion or respect.

Martha was very upset that I did not accept that position, and continued to give me a hard time. It left me no choice but to contact Human Resources and request short term disability. She was not happy with the decision but through this office I was approved for 3 months and guaranteed that my job would still be there when I returned. They further advised her that this behavior was not acceptable and changes needed to be made.

After I returned to work I felt things would be different. The management had not changed. Louis and Fanny still remained as supervisors. They continued to hassle the co-workers.

All the staff had to continually defend themselves against actions that were not in their control. Like the rest of the co-workers I wasn't ready to throw in the towel. We felt Human Resources should have done more to resolve the ongoing issues.

Martha continued to display favoritism. When any of the employees had a birthday, she always bought a big cake and sometimes gave that person a nice gift. I never expected anything and treated it as another day in my life.

On one occasion after a staff meeting and a day after my birthday, Fanny took a dried up muffin, put a candle on it and handed it to me. It was like a slap in the face. I would have been happier if she had done nothing.

I just looked at the muffin and walked out of the room as it upset me. Fanny followed me and said you didn't eat your muffin. I told her what to do with it and also that she only embarrassed herself with what she did.

At meetings we were always asked to come up with suggestions to improve things in the office. I always came up with suggestions that were good but they were not appreciated. Then a few days or weeks later, someone else reproduced my suggestion and was rewarded for it. They often used my suggestions but I never got credit for them. Martha usually bought token gifts to reward these people.

The office needed a new collector for the open position and Jenny joined us. She seemed to have a good personality, and was helpful at first but then things seemed to change.

She tried to get me to socialize with her after hours. I went with her to several events and she always questioned me about a lot of things pertaining to work. I began to feel suspicious and declined other outings.

I did not own a computer and did not know how to use one. None of the previous firms I worked for supplied computers to incumbents. The co-workers were advised that the firm was upgrading and the employees would have a computer to work on.

A representative from the computer company came in and advised when he would be installing the computers and that there would be one on every desk. After they installed the computers, we were advised someone would come in and give us some instructions as the collectors accounts would all be on the computers.

The representative only spent one and a half days showing 12 people how to operate the computers. In his opinion, there were enough experienced people on staff.

When I requested help from Martha, she declined. She said; "figure it out yourself". I did learn to open and close but often I had problems with the password. Since I had not taken computer courses it was hard to even follow the written instructions. I had to change my password often but I managed to open the computer.

Before I got the hang of it, I had opened and closed many times. Jenny was helpful to me because she was a little more experienced with computers as she had been exposed to them. She always assisted when I asked her for help.

I don't know if they thought I was a "superwoman" but on many occasions Fanny wanted me to handle 2-3 desks during certain periods when others were away and expected me keep the desks up to date. It would have been impossible even for her to handle all the desks.

I tried my best and even worked a lot of overtime to accommodate them but was told there was no payment for overtime. I tried to discuss this with Martha but was unsuccessful in achieving any results.

I requested permission to take a few night courses pertaining to management skills that the firm offered but management declined. They chose to pay for others but I was told I would be responsible for the costs.

Due to the situation in our office, I quit socializing with this crew. When I attended previous gatherings, they always wanted to split the bill equally. The problem was I only had one drink and some had many, it just didn't seem fair.

The staff was then reduced to 8 employees and we were informed that there would be changes. They transferred accounts from other provinces for us to handle. Their plan was to eventually close those branches. We were informed our workloads would increase. At this time, I had already spent 12 years with this firm, accumulated some benefits, and decided to stay.

After coaching, managing and recruiting players for many years, I decided to take a break from the sport. I had been involved with ladies fastball for over 20 years. My husband and I decided to fold the team.

We found it hard to get commitments from players and sometimes were short of players. One of the players and her husband decided to keep the team and managed it for several years. After a couple of years the team folded but we did not feel bad as we had a lot of good memories. We are still friends with this couple and their twin daughters.

We were on our way to a Provincial Tournament in Lloyminister, the year, there was a tornado in the Edmonton area. We noticed a funnel cloud forming in front of us at a distance. Once we realized what it was, we detoured arriving late at our destination and it was raining in the town. When we went through Camrose there was at least 2-3 inches of hail on the ground.

We ended up playing later in the evening and kept warm by drinking hot chocolate and doing the line dance. We came home with a Silver medal from that tournament. During our reign, we entered several Provincial Tournaments and earned three silver medals for our efforts.

My husband had a small 20 ft. camper and we did a lot of camping at Mount Kidd in Kananaskis and the Canyon campground as we both enjoyed the outdoors.

Originally, we stored the camper at our friend's acreage and when we purchased a bigger home with a big back yard, we moved it to the city. It was handier to have it closer to home.

With my husband being a referee, he participated at many hockey tournaments and we were able to travel to many different places. One year we flew to St. John, NB. and spent just over a week there. After the tournament, we were fortunate to tour the city with the organizers. There was branch of our firm near the hotel and I was able to visit and meet some of the staff.

We returned to Toronto and continued on to San Diego. We carried a lot of baggage that year, winter clothes to N.B and summer clothes to San Diego. After spending two weeks in this part of the country, we headed home via Los Angeles.

We made a number of trips to Florida, mostly to Daytona Beach. We did a lot of tanning, walked the beach looking for star fish, and then did pub crawls at night. We had some real good times there and I was even brave enough to drive the rented car. It turned out to be a very friendly place. We also went to Orlando, saw Disneyworld, Tampa Bay and Miami and toured many other parts.

We also attended several tournaments in Las Vegas during the winter. One of the tournaments was held just outside of Las Vegas at a small community. We stayed at the hotel which was connected to a hockey rink, a bowling alley and of course a casino. On the next trip we stayed at the Sands hotel which has now been demolished.

The following year we went to Montreal and my husband able to referee in the old NHL rink, the Montreal Forum. We met with the famous Maurice Richard and got autographs. We befriended some of the Russian players who participated in the tournament and I was able to converse with them a bit.

We also attended a tournament in Toronto where we met a lot of the older NHL players from both teams who played in the 1972 game against Russia. I visited several the branches from our firm. I had the opportunity to have lunch with the sponsor of my ball team and thanked him personally for his sponsorship. We attended our first basketball game (Raptors) in Toronto.

There were annual tournaments held in Victoria and Vancouver and we were able to attend many of them. My husband did the games and I often volunteered befriending many people. We sometimes visited families in both of the cities, his aunt lived in Sooke, B.C. and we always made a point to see her.

In 1988 the Olympics were in our city, some of us wanted to volunteer but were not given permission to do so until it was too late. My husband was able to arrange time off and volunteered with hockey.

In that year we also took a trip to Europe. The Referee Association from Ottawa scheduled a hockey tournament in Germany with teams attending from different countries. They were able to get us a good deal on the flight and accommodations so we decided to make the trip.

While in Munich, we went to visit other countries. Our mother came from Austria as a young girl and I wanted to see her birth place. We took the train from Germany and went to Salzburg, Austria. That was the place where they filmed the show "Sound of Music". We visited the filming area and the gazebo. It was very interesting and we saw some churches where the ceiling was made with gold.

We took a few tours in Germany and the cable cars were the most fun. In the cars were mostly people from Canada. They served us pretzels, radishes and beer. Each person getting off the cable car was given a huge mug of beer. Here you were allowed to walk on the street carrying your drinks. I did not drink beer but my husband insisted I take it anyway, and it did not go to waste.

After one social gathering for the teams in Germany, we agreed to meet friends by the Opera House. While sitting on the steps of the Opera House in Munich, my husband wanted to sing there, we convinced him not to.

While at a beer house in Munich a young man said he would take our picture for $8.00 Canadian and send it to us. At first I thought it was a scam but agreed to pay him the $8.00. Three weeks after returning to Canada we received two pictures from him and they were great.

After the tournament, we rented a car and stayed mostly in Bed & Breakfast places as they were cheaper. We saw 8 countries and drove 1500 miles in the 3 weeks we were there including Switzerland, Luxemburg and Holland. Zurich is very mountainous.

On one of our camping trips we decided to take my goddaughter's young daughter camping. The great niece was 3 yrs old, mature for her age and spoke well. We placed her at the foot of our bed to sleep so we could keep an eye on her.

She got up very early the next morning and just sat quietly at the end of the bed waiting for us to get up. My husband realized she was up and asked what was wrong. She calmly said, I think my mom packed another pair of pajamas, we knew what she meant. I dealt with the problem and we went back to sleep.

After breakfast she told me to stay inside and do the dishes while she went outside. I could only come out when she told me I could. She made my husband build a fire and she put the chairs around the fire.

She came to the door and knocked, then, she said "Cinderella you can come out now".

I burst out laughing as I could not believe what she came up with. Then she said to my husband you have to dance with Cinderella. He said to her there is no music to dance to. She quickly responded I will be your music. She walked around the chairs and hummed a tune.

My husband and I did not want to disappoint her so we complied with her request. We danced by the fire for a few minutes. The neighboring campers must have thought we were a strange couple dancing at 10:00 AM in the morning in front of a fire.

When this great niece was born she was so small it was hard to find clothes for her. I purchased some Cabbage Patch Patterns and used them to make clothes for her. She still has the bunting bag I made and now will be using for her own daughter.

On another camping trip, we ended up taking her and her younger sister. The younger girl was also well spoken for her age approx. 3yrs old. She was asleep when we reached the campground. We didn't want to wake her so we carried her in.

We laid her down where she was going to be sleeping and tried to tuck her in. She opened her eyes and said "Why are you fussing so much over me I'm okay".

The next day while having supper she quietly said "I don't know if I should say this at the dinner table. Then she said "This is the life". After the camping trip she said she would save all her money in the piggy bank to buy a motor home.

We will always treasure these memories.

With reference to the girls' parents and while my niece was living with me, we decided to have a Ukrainian Christmas party. She had just met a new fellow and we invited him to help with the preparations.

We made the traditional 12 dishes and the bread known as the "Kolach". After the dough was made, we let him braid the dough and place it in a circle. He then decorated it with birds made of dough. The birds on this dough decided to lie down.

We decided to give door prizes for the fun ot it. We shopped at a Ukrainian store. The clerks were very friendly and helpful, they even lent us their Ukrainian blouses to wear.

The first prize was "Rubber Boots" and fun was had by all. My niece ended up marrying this fellow.

Chapter Twelve

In 1991 they decided to establish a centralized office in our city for collections. The manager would have to take special training to be able to handle a large volume of accounts and a large staff. The position was offered to Martha and she accepted. She was then, advised she would be going out of town for 3 years to train, at another centralized office.

While she was going to be away, she appointed Louis as the acting manager and Fanny as the acting supervisor. This was a mistake as they were both not qualified to run the office.

After Martha left they both became very demanding and started putting unnecessary pressure on all the co-workers. They did not seem to work with all the people there but rather against. Perhaps they should have been sent for training before being handed these positions.

They made their own rules about doing the employee reviews. Their opinion of a good supervisor was finding faults with the incumbents' work and not dwelling on the good they did for the firm. They claimed they would be focusing on what the co-workers did wrong. They also stated the future reviews would be based on these points, as they wanted to be recognized by Human Resources.

I had never heard this before and certainly felt they were not handling their duties professionally. There was something terribly wrong with this picture. If I could figure it out why couldn't they. It made it hard for us to respect someone with this type of attitude and they certainly were not aware of their misdoings.

For some unknown reason Fanny was not fond of Irma and continued to upset people she did not like. Irma was well liked by the co-workers, had a nice personality and was easy to get along with. Her husband worked for a radio station and they had no family so she often put in extra time.

Jenny and Fanny became good friends and seemed to spend a lot of time together. However, we found it hard to trust Jenny as it seemed she spent a lot of time with both Louis and Fanny in meetings.

In spite of all the mishaps, the co-workers tolerated both supervisors and chose not to quit over misunderstandings while Martha was away. Louis always seemed to involve himself in unpleasant situations usually in front of other staff. Some of co-workers tolerated this until a certain point and then they filed complaints with Human Resources.

Often these situations were very embarrassing for the rest of us and we found it hard to be respectful to these individuals involved. When the complaints were actually filed, the management was always disappointed that things went that far, but did nothing to resolve the issues.

After their discussions were over, Louis would sheepishly apologize to the others claiming he had a bad day. Unfortunately, his good days were very limited. At one point, I was told I wasn't allowed to joke with him without permission.

Maybe I should have booked an appointment when I wanted to tell him a joke. I chose to look the other way and ignore his behavior as I was not interested in joking with him. However, he claimed he would discuss issues pertaining to the accounts.

A few weeks later another unpleasant situation occurred, this time the person did not get involved in any discussion and went directly to the complaint department. He accused me of encouraging her to do what she did. I informed him, since he created the problem, it was up to him to resolve it.

Upon receiving the complaint, they sent out an investigator to interview the staff and to determine why these problems kept recurring. The investigator became aware the problems were multiplying and tried to make recommendations. They chose to call me at home to discuss my views as they did not want me to be intimidated by management.

Although both of the acting management personnel were warned about their behavior, they chose to ignore their warnings. Disciplining them did not seem to work as they did not take it seriously.

Human Resources staff seemed to show sympathy towards the matter but did not resolve it, all they did was put a bandage on the situation and hoped it would eventually go away but it didn't. The best solution to resolve this matter was, to remove the problem completely.

Later that week, Human Resources sent out a survey requesting suggestions as to how to ease the tension and improve the morale at this office. Our suggestion was unanimous, we requested they recruit a strong leader with a good attitude and willing to deal fairly with co-workers. We needed a change and the present leaders did not fit the bill.

After the surveys were completed and returned to them no changes were made and the problem did not get resolved. As a result that survey was a waste of time and money and the money could have been better spent. They did not succeed in removing the bandage.

My husband had family in Port Alberni so we attended the Summer Games there in 1992. The family had two boys and a girl. One of the boys competed in the games in water skiing. They lived near a lake and the whole family participated in water skiing.

Since Martha would be returning soon, the acting management attempted to ease of the pressure and showed the co-workers a little respect. They did not want any more complaints before Martha returned as they knew she would not be impressed.

Upon Martha's return, she informed us we will require a bigger office and the number of co-workers would increase to approximately 12-15. While Martha was trying to find a new location, she accepted applications from people who wanted to transfer and other interested parties. She allowed the acting management to assist with the applications.

Often Fanny would give me instructions to relay to the others and later she would recant in front of them and deny those instructions. Perhaps she was trying to embarrass me. I got wise to her and from then on I requested all the instructions be in writing.

When she tried to say I gave the wrong instructions, I would take out her instructions and hand them to her. Her response was, she had forgotten that she gave those instructions but did not apologize. She only embarrassed herself.

We continued to camp at Mount Kidd, but sometimes it was hard to get the sites you wanted on long weekends. The campground was becoming very popular with both Canadian and American tourists. To get a spot at that time, you could only phone on a particular day.

My husband and I spent hours, and sometimes days, to get through using 3 phones but we managed to get a spot not always what we wanted. On one of the trips, my niece and her husband from out of town joined us for the weekend. The camper was crowded but we managed. After several trips with us they chose to rent a small trailer and bring their family.

The following years, our little group increased slowly and we ended up getting 4 spots adjacent to each other and camped as a group for a number of years. My sister and her family had a camper while some nieces and nephews who had no campers stayed in tents. We usually had 18 or more people on the weekend.

During the weekend most the families cooked their own meals. We often shared breakfasts and sometimes we had potluck supper with everyone meeting at one place. On occasion, other family members joined us for a meal including my husband's family.

During the day the group usually hiked, biked and played several games that were available at the park. In the evening we had a big camp fire and sat around as a group. There were sing-songs and a lot of joke telling among the group. We often played cards using the camping lamps for light.

On one occasion a group of us hiked to the Ribbon Creek Falls approx.10 kilometers away. On the way back it rained and we were soaked before we got back.

We also walked up the Indefatigable Mountain. I walked most of the way but some of the hikers went to the top. I stayed behind as my niece got tired and did not want to go any further.

Also there were always a few of the crowd that took a drive to Banff to go shopping, as it was not that far from the campsite during the weekend. Occasionally we went to Radium campground on our own or tried other parks.

While camping at Mount Kidd on one weekend we had a young moose come to our RV. He stared through our window as we ate. We advised the Wild Life Warden but the moose was not anxious to leave the spot beside our trailer. Eventually they got him to leave after many efforts.

While we camped at Radium, we often golfed even though we were not good golfers. We also participated in small tournaments held by his co-workers.

On one occasion, I was on a team with 3 fairly good golfers. When it came to the 9th hole, I let them go first. They all putted but missed putting the ball in the hole.

Now the pressure was on me. I surveyed the situation and hit the ball hoping it would head for the hole. To my surprise, it rolled right to the hole which was approximately 35 feet away and downhill.

My team jumped with joy and the spectators on the side of the hill cheered. By making this putt, it put our team in first place. I was proud of the accomplishment and received a nice prize.

Chapter Thirteen

Martha found a new location and the office would soon be moving again. The arrangements were to move in November of 1994, new staff had to be arranged to fill the newly created positions.

Martha along with Louis began interviewing each person in the office for their positions at the new location. The co-workers were informed if they did not wish to transfer they were welcome to make their own arrangements. They also interviewed the new potential prospects.

I was looking forward to moving to the new location. I handled the same position for the past three years and managed to get the work done satisfactorily. Since I had spent so many years in this line of work I wasn't about to change.

When my turn came, Martha informed me she was willing to transfer me to the other location but I would have to accept a lower position. At that point I was not aware she was trying to discourage me from transferring by offering a lower position. I was disappointed in their approach and walked out.

After several lengthy discussions with both Martha and Louis, I informed them I was not prepared to accept lower position or quit at this time. I basically said if they had no lateral position for me, they may want to fire me as the ball was in their court and returned to my desk.

A couple hours later Louis came to my desk and handed me a job description and asked me to review it. I picked up the document without reading it, placed it on his desk and informed him, if he felt I didn't qualify he could offer it to someone else as I wasn't changing my decision.

Martha did not discuss the situation any further and nothing was said. While waiting for the new location to be ready Martha suggested some the co-workers take staggered holidays. She wanted most of the staff there when the office relocated. I already had plans so I agreed to take mine.

While I was on holidays apparently Fanny was job hunting for me without my permission. Upon my return I was informed that she had some exciting news for me. For the life of me I had no idea what she was talking about and listened to what she had to say.

She spoke up and said I found you a new job. I know you will like it, and it is a lateral move. I informed her I was not looking for a job when I went on vacation and am not looking for one now, as I had one. If she thought it was such a good position maybe she should have considered it.

While I was away, Jonas decided not to accept the transfer and was looking into retirement. He attended the Human Resources office, and worked out a suitable package. Then he advised Martha, he would not be accepting the position.

Upon learning of his decision, Martha became upset as they needed someone experienced to fill his position and did not have time to train anyone. She held a meeting with her assistants and decided to offer me the position. Within a few days I was demoted and promoted back to a qualifying position. At this point they needed me not the opposite.

It is now Nov. 1994 and we made the move to the new location. We were located on third floor of this downtown office and were in the same building as payroll and Human Resources. We had a lot of new co-workers who were not experienced and some were green in this line of work.

I was asked to train one of the new co-workers who accepted the job I turned down. I spent three weeks training her but she did not pan out. She had made arrangements for vacation while accepting the position. When she returned from vacation, she applied for sick leave and did not return.

Combining four offices proved to be a big job as the accounts were transferred from different provinces and different rules applied. Everything had to be properly recorded and logged. The new staff required lots of training and this created many backlogs.

They offered to pay overtime, while the office was being organized and everything was running smoothly. Not everyone volunteered to work overtime. I felt I had the experience so I agreed to help out after working hours. I made sure I recorded my overtime and had it initialed by a supervisor. Some days I worked 8-8 and accumulated over 300 hours in overtime but at times no appreciation was shown.

The move did not go smoothly, after we moved they decided to do more renovations and this created havoc on the backlog. The office had to be closed and the staff was advised they had to make up the time, or they could take vacation time.

It is now Feb.1995, and Fanny was assigned to do my review. She gave me an above average rating and I was impressed. She thanked me in writing how much she appreciated that I helped with the backlog and worked overtime. She was happy I helped organize the office. I was beginning to think that maybe she had a change of heart as she acted differently. I soon found out that was not the case.

For a short time, the duties in the department were divided between three people and that seemed to work fine. Then they allowed several people to take vacations the same time which left a number of desks with no one on them. They advised me I was expected to cover three desks which included mine and try to keep everything up to date. This was impossible and they knew it.

In private, Fanny intimated me, and said since I was unable to handle all the desks, she was obligated to give a lower rating. On the previous review she stated she was so impressed, she even bought a pet rock which said "Thanks for a job well done".

After this interview, she complained she was out pocket money for the rock. I went to my desk picked up the rock and said to her if you take the rock back you may be able to retrieve your money. Since I was not happy with the review I filed a rebuttal. Martha refused to get involved, advised me to deal with Fanny and threatened me about losing my job.

After performing all the extra duties, I developed tendonitis which later turned to carpal tunnel syndrome. My family doctor gave me some medication, a brace to put on my hand and suggested some therapy. The pain and the swelling of my hand made it impossible for me to button up my own clothes. This of course stressed me out and I was constantly pressured with extra workloads.

As my medical problems increased I suggested that I should be placed on short term disability but they refused. They accused me of faking the illness and wearing a fake brace pretending to have a problem and continued to badger me.

Even with the medication and brace the pain did not subside so my doctor referred me to a specialist at the hand clinic. After the examination, he advised me the tendonitis turned to carpal tunnel syndrome and they needed to operate to reduce the pressure. He suggested I go on sick leave until the swelling goes down.

Upon returning to the office I referred the letter with his recommendation to Fanny. She flatly refused to co-operate, threw the letter at me and then responded by saying "come and see me when you are really sick".

The specialist suggested I try a different brace and advised me the hospital would make it for me. When I returned from the hospital, I was informed I would lose pay as I took unnecessary time off. I just did not understand their reaction to my illness. They all saw the condition of my hand and the swelling but looked the other way.

I became frustrated because I did have letters from the family doctor, the specialist and therapist, yet I was not allowed to apply for short term disability according to management. I had no choice but file those documents with Human Resources and request their assistance.

Only when Human Resources contacted them, they agreed to acknowledge my illness. They placed an envelope on desk with insurance forms and a letter. I was not impressed, they saw I had a problem for approximately four months which they ignored and now they were sorry to hear I was sick.

I had the forms completed which cost me $50.00 and I brought them to the office but they were not sent in to the insurance company as promised. Only after I contacted the insurance company I realized what was going on. A few days later the insurance company called and advised they received the forms but did not appreciate the branch comments.

The comments came from Fanny who stated I was faking the illness, wearing false braces and paid the doctors to write fake letters. Between the Human Resources office and the insurance company, they agreed to authorize 6 months leave instead of 3. The investigation showed that this situation was very poorly handled. They also stated my job was guaranteed.

Perhaps I should have exercised my rights and taken the appropriate action, but I chose not to at that time.

Chapter Fourteen

Upon my return in December of 1995, I was assigned a new supervisor and made him aware of my situation. He attempted to give good reviews but they always resulted in rebuttals. Again the manager advised she was not getting involved.

She liked to have contests for the staff. Quizzes were her favorite at meetings. She often gave out small gifts to all people who won except me so I stopped participating in them.

In July of 1996, the surgeon advised that he could now do the operation. My right hand seemed worse than the left so he did the right hand first and then in November of 1996 he did the other hand. I went on short term disability again.

The branch was raising funds for United Way and decided to have a few contests. I won the first contest with wearing the Wackiest Hat, got a golf shirt and then won a $50.00 gift certificate in another contest which surprised me.

By January I guess I had been pushing it too hard again my problem reoccurred. I developed a lump on my right hand, the doctor gave cortisone shots to ease the pain, and said I required new braces. I went on disability again until the swelling went down and the hospital was able to make new braces.

I befriended Ginny who transferred in from an out of town office. She was very helpful and had a good personality. Her family was scattered between two provinces and after a death in her family she requested a transfer to the other province but of course she was refused.

She chose to apply elsewhere and was accepted at a position where she would be making more money and a promotion. She was handed a small token gift but not much was said to her.

The payroll department had vacated their office which was larger than ours, and regional office allowed us to move to that office. At that time they also closed several collections branches in other cities and their plan was to handle all accounts out of our office.

Martha managed the office at the new location for a short time but she was not comfortable after all that happened. She chose to take a position that was out the country in a foreign office. Fanny was transferred to a northern office. Louis remained in the branch

Before Martha left, she gave me approval to take the management course which was paid for by Human Resources. The course was at the University as evening classes. I managed to pass the course with a high mark of over 80% which really surprised Martha.

One of the new incumbents was Hilda, married with a family of two boys. She was very close to her dad and when he became ill, it really stressed her out. She seemed very friendly at first when I befriended her then she changed.

Mark was a single father, supported a 12 year old son and came to us from a different branch. Then Rita joined us, married with a family and a husband with an illness. Later her daughter joined the firm also. All seemed to go well for a short time.

Horace arrived to replace Martha as manager. He had spent a lot of time in the executive office and his management experience was limited. He was not what we were anticipating for that position. Louis remained as his assistant and Elmer transferred in from another city. Elmer then became the junior supervisor.

Chapter Fifteen

It was 1998, and my reviews would now to be done by Elmer. I worked hard, never took sick days, handled duties for others when they were away and he refused to give me good reviews again the rebuttals came in play. His excuse was his supervisor would not allow it.

In my duties I managed to handle 65 or more collection accounts daily, over 1,258 monthly, over 100 pieces of paper weekly, prepared special reports and stats as requested, handled many calls from customers, solicitors agents and accommodated these people as required.

After several discussions pertaining to one of the rebuttals, I was informed I was doing an excellent job verbally by Elmer but he could not put it in writing after that many rebuttals followed, as a result of these reviews, I received lower raises and bonus.

After receiving one of the rebuttals, Horace, the manager suggested that Elmer and I sign a contract between us, which stated I would accept all Elmer's decisions on my reviews. It was a ridiculous suggestion, I declined it, then advised Human Resources office of the issue.

In the spring of 1999, Ben, from the Human Resources office, attempted to resolve the issue. Being unsuccessful, he chose to move Horace back to the executive office. Obviously the problem was not resolved but only compounded.

As a referee, my husband got invited to the Snoopy tournament which was held in July every year in Santa Rosa, California. Several referees went from Canada and made a vacation out of the trip. Originally, they only accommodated the referees, then later, they included the families.

This tournament was run and sponsored by Charles Shultz. He was the creator of the comic strips of Snoopy, Lucy, Charlie Brown and many others. Mr. Schultz has since left us but we will always remember him and what he accomplished.

Originally he built a skating rink and then it was used as a hockey rink. He loved his hockey and held tournaments. Teams were invited from Canada, USA and Europe. The tournament was split in to age groups. He played in the 70"s group. We talked to him on many occasions and obtained autographs.

We usually took an extra week off for the trip as we were driving to Santa Rosa and also made a holiday out of the trip. We did this for approximately 15 years. It was an enjoyable trip each time. We made many friends, and it was our yearly holiday. After my husband had knee surgery instead of refereeing, he assisted with time keeping and other duties.

The wives usually passed the time together and when it was convenient we all met as a group for meals in the evenings. We have many great memories from these trips and of the people we met. We also have lots of Snoopy mementos at our house.

While in Santa Rosa we visited San Francisco several times and took in the San Francisco Giants games. On one of our trips, my older sister and my youngest sister, joined us and were able to see one of the games.

While at the Snoopy tournament, we made friends with a couple from Oakland. Later, on one of the trips, we left home a few days earlier and spent some time with them. We also took in an Oakland A's game that year.

On the last trip we took to Santa Rosa, my youngest sister joined us on the trip. We also stopped at Oakland to see one of their games. They gave out team jerseys to the fans that particular game, so we came home with the A's jerseys.

We toured many wineries in this area and often bought wine to take home. Kendall Jackson was one of the bigger ones we toured. The tour guide on one of trips had a wagon and two horses and took us through the actual wine fields which he had access to.

While we checked out the wine sampling at one of the wineries, the driver prepared a picnic for our group outside the building. The lunch included crackers, cheese, strawberries and a bottle of wine.

We always enjoyed both the trips and the tours and drove to the tournament, as a vehicle was required for transportation there. We travelled through Lethbridge,

Shelby, Great Falls,Helena, Butte, Dillion, Idaho Falls and stopped at Pocatello for the night.

The next morning, we continued by Twin Falls, Wells Nev., Elko, Winnemucca, Lovelock, and stayed at Reno one or two nights. From there we went by Weed, Redding, Vacaville, Sacramento, Fairfield entered Napa Valley and headed on to Santa Rosa.

On the way back we often changed our trip route. We stayed at Redding a few times, and while there we visited Mount Shasta and the famous caves.

I am claustrophobic and do not like small compact places but I am glad I was able to see the caves. It was a little scary and compact when you first enter but once you get to the big caves it gets better. We had a good guide and found it very interesting.

Other times we went through Spokane and spent some time at Bonner's Ferry and Sandpont. We also enjoyed spending some time in Bend and Portland. We even detoured to Victoria on one trip and took the Port Angeles Ferry when my husband's aunt lived there. She has since passed on and will always be remembered.

Chapter Sixteen

The new manager replacing Horace was Wilma. Since I worked with her previously, I was hoping I would have a better relationship with her this round.

When she first arrived, it appeared that she might be more approachable at this time but this wasn't the case. Eventually she started picking favorites and this upset many co-workers. Even if you had a heavy work load and helped make the office successful little appreciation was shown.

She did not appreciate staff that had been involved with situations that pertained to Human Resources. She was fully aware of the complaints I filed but she showed little remorse towards what happened. Like Martha she was playing the same rules. If anyone was not happy with her decisions, they should not complain to Human Resources but rather move on.

Wilma was a great party person and had many favorite night clubs. Occasionally she asked the whole office to join her, but many declined. When she had a bad night we always knew as it reflected on her behavior the next day.

Hilda tried to be friends with everyone but always tried to fraternize with management, soon Rita did the same. Perhaps they were trying for brownie points with management.

At this time, we no longer had a receptionist. Debra who worked part time at the main branch transferred to our office as receptionist / secretary. She was a good typist and was an asset to the branch. She had an excellent personality and certainly possessed management skills.

Carmen joined her on part time basis and helped with the receptionist work. Debra always tried to console me when I had a bad day. Carla who previously worked at Head Office joined us for a short time. She was very friendly, helpful and never let you down. Her husband was a radio announcer so she was well known to many.

She had great management skills and handled matters in a very professional manner. I was befriended by all three and we still remain friends. I was sorry to see her go when she left.

Maggie worked for a short time with a handicap (eyesight) problem. She was pleasant and tried to please the co-workers. She was only assigned miscellaneous duties. Management did not like her and weeded her out.

At one of the staff meeting it was decided that we form a social fund with the staff putting in $10.00 a month. They decided to make it payroll deduction with few additional collections. The price of a gift would depend on the amount of time in the office.

The funds were mishandled from the beginning and funds soon ran out. Shortly after the social fund was formed, two ladies who worked a short time with us due to becoming pregnant were rewarded handsomely. They got baby carriages and miscellaneous items. They even bought the women night gowns along with the expensive baby gifts.

Several people who went on sick leave, off and on, received $100.00 worth of flowers each time they went on sick leave. When several co-workers had family pass away, they sent flowers on behalf of the co-workers and this drained the fund very fast.

They even held a doggy shower for an employee who purchased a new puppy, because it was someone Wilma liked. She was also a bird lover, it's a wonder we did not have bird showers.

I had been with firm for a number of years now. Every time someone had a birthday, they always got a cake and token gift. It was now my 60th birthday, a milestone birthday. I didn't expect much to happen because in the past I was lucky to get a birthday card left on my desk.

After a short meeting I was informed by Hilda they had a gift for me to celebrate my birthday. Jenny presented me with a small nicely wrapped box. As I opened it, I was so stunned as to what I saw in the box. They actually bought me a; "crummy crystal ashtray". Then Hilda commented, that it was all they could afford, and I did not understand why she made that comment.

I inquired as to why they bought this type of gift, as no one in my family smoked. Jenny suggested I use it for a candy dish. I was so heartbroken I left the ashtray there and went home. The next day, I found it on my desk, I put it on the filing cabinet and stayed there until the office closed. I was tempted to use it for a frizz-bee. They would have been better off giving me nothing because they only embarrassed themselves.

My husband and I spent 14 years together before getting married and it happened in July 1999. We had been on a trip to California and on the way back we stopped in Vegas. Upon my return I told my new supervisor and the manager about the marriage.

My new supervisor was now Nina who transferred in from another branch and Wilma was impressed with her from the beginning. They soon became good friends.

Nina told me that she would arrange a meeting in August so they could present me with a wedding gift. This never happened and the co-workers were disappointed.

By now I had been with this firm over 20 years and with the department since 1984, but received little acknowledgement and not even a card. We had 14 + employees at the branch at that time.

After a weekly meeting, Hilda stood up and sheepishly said we would like to give you a wedding gift and handed me an envelope. She made it worse by stating that was all they could afford, a gift certificate to the store next door. (60.00). I was disappointed but said nothing and walked away.

Wilma liked her night life but didn't always have good mornings and snapped at people when it wasn't necessary. She often tried to take her frustrations out on me.

A month or so later, a fairly new employee was getting married and they decided to collect for his wedding gift. He was leaving the branch, going to a different department and in the process of getting married.

Hilda and Jenny asked the co-workers to contribute $20.00 per person as the social fund was dry. I had already cancelled my membership with the social fund and declined this request. It turned out they bought Gerry an expensive barbecue worth $500.00 +. A few days later Gerry apologized.

The social butterfly liked to attract attention and during Stampede week, she invited the staff to join her at a local pub across the street. Several people went and I joined them. I felt the behavior was in appropriate so I left.

For a while things went smoothly, co-workers were treated with respect and the pressure was reduced. Nina now did my reviews but I ran into the same problems and again there were rebuttals as Wilma did not agree with Nina's comments.

Most of the male staff members were married and not interested in bar hopping. However, she managed to convince Mark to join her on occasion. He was in his mid 30's, divorced and supporting a young son. She was much older but they became good friends.

She bought a new SUV and liked to brag about it because she had a place to sleep if she was unable to drive. Strangely, a few weeks later Mark got a promotion, a big raise and his desk was moved to the front of the office.

One day while we were having a meeting his son decided to meet him at work. As he came through the door, he walked over to her and said nice to see you again. The room sort of went silent and everyone dispersed. She went back to her office and he just left.

He phoned in sick the next day and stayed away for a couple of days. When he returned he had his resignation ready and handed it in. He was offered a transfer but he declined.

Most of the Christmas dinners were held at a designated restaurant with staff and their spouses. That particular year Wilma suggested that we eat at the office.

It seemed like a good idea at the time and it was cheaper. We had a large lunch room and could have a pot luck dinner. She cooked the turkey, assigned other people to bring different dishes and she agreed to supply the wine.

After a few glasses of the red stuff, the social butterfly opened up. Her comments were best not repeated, and the majority walked out with their plates. They felt the comments were in bad taste.

In the fall of 2002, head office made a decision to move all the accounts to the office down east. All the collections would be done from that office. The office was almost fully staffed and not many transfers were made available.

All the staff stayed until the office was actually closed a number of months later. There were only 2-3 interested in moving down east and our office tried to accommodate them.

One of the co-workers that was accepted for transfer was a single mom separated from her husband. Her parents lived in that city and were able to assist with babysitting. The second just wanted a change and to try elsewhere.

With approximately 15 co-workers left, they were offered several different options which included retirement packages, transfers or temporary positions with partial packages. I weighed the pros and cons and since I was eligible for retirement, I decided to accept the package.

Jenny took a position at the new Centre and a couple others joined her. Louis took a transfer as he was not eligible for retirement. Wilma accepted a temporary position. Elmer and several others took the six month deal. Debra returned to her part time branch and Carla took a position elsewhere.

Before the office closed Human Resources sent an employee from down east to assist people with resumes and discuss the options they had. Then Ben came around, an executive I dealt with earlier to help with the closing and answer questions.

Wilma would not allow anyone to talk to Ben alone. When my turn came I declined because what I had to say was confidential.

Unfortunately I did not get to speak to Ben alone, but at this point, it no longer mattered, as the office was closing. There was no departing party as most had left.

Over the years, we have made many trips to the original homestead, where my brother and his family live.

On one of the trips, we went berry picking and I got stung by wasps. I sat on a log to pick berries and got bit on the behind and under my right eye.

By morning my face was swollen and my eye shut. They took me to the local hospital, and the first thing the nurse said was; Who beat her up??. We laughed but it really wasn't funny as I was in pain.

They gave me a shot and some medication. When the swelling went down I was again able to wear my contacts.

Chapter Seventeen

Approximately 5-6 months after taking retirement, I started to look for work and found a receptionist job at an agency that was doing work for our firm at one time.

I scheduled an interview. When I met with the manager, he said he would not hire me as a receptionist with my experience but rather as a collector. He agreed to pay me salary plus commission and I took the offer. Some months I cleared double what I got at the previous job. I had almost two and a half years before the government pensions kicked in. I decided to bide my time here.

It was approximately 2-3 weeks before my 65th birthday, the office announced they would be closing that office and moving all accounts to the nearby city to cut costs. It was time to pack it in and give up this line of work. I got offers from other agencies but I declined them.

Since I was leaving the workforce and my 65th birthday was due shortly, it certainly was time for a celebration.

My niece (godchild) suggested we have a party at her house. It was July, she had a swimming pool and it was a nice weekend. The party was Hawaiian theme and everyone dressed accordingly. Some family came from out of town plus friends. We all had a good time.

Since it was a milestone birthday, I had a video made showing memories from childhood. I received many nice gifts. I hope my three godchildren will remember me through this video. My godson's wife was pregnant and was due shortly. After spending a lot of time in the pool, she delivered early (a girl). It was 2 days after my birthday. They have a boy and a girl. The 3rd godchild did not attend.

After retirement, we travelled a bit and went to Hawaii several times. My younger sister participated in running marathons and she ran three in Hawaii. The marathons were 43 miles and she handled it. Of course she had trained for many years prior. We went there to watch her come in after the race and also made it a vacation. On our last trip to Hawaii in 2008, I chose to participate in their 10 km walk.

After I finished the walk, I wished I would have registered to go further because I felt I could have handled it. Prior to coming to Hawaii I trained for months and walked many miles daily. However, it was the participation that really counted as there were over 25,000 people participating some years. I also have a short video on this walk, which I could look back on and reminisce.

Since my husband and I were both involved with softball and baseball, we became interested in the new local baseball team that was formed in our city called "The Vipers". They stayed around for a few years but due to lack of support the team folded. I often volunteered at the games. We attended mostly all their games except when we were out of town.

Due to the weather changes here, it did not help the team. Fans were not supporting this sport, and financially the team could not manage. The Cannons were here prior to the Vipers.

While the team existed we travelled a bit to see the team play out of town. We saw a number of games in Edmonton, Victoria and also travelled to Orange County, Chico, and Tucson. We befriended one of the players who invited us to visit them in Phoenix.

We also had relatives on my husband's side at Yuma. They had their own place there. So we planned a trip for three weeks and drove there. We spent a week in Yuma with his cousin and her husband. We visited other friends lived there too.

Then we headed to Phoenix to spend the rest of our holiday. We stayed there with a ball player we befriended from the Vipers team and his family.

We went to some spring training games. Met a lot of his wife's relatives and had some good times. We also visited people we knew from our city who had places there. It was a good holiday. On the way home we spent a couple days in Las Vegas.

Three years ago our grandson, who is 9 now, decided he wanted to play hockey. We enrolled him and he has been playing ever since. First two years he played defense and this year he decided he wanted to be a goalie and has taken a lot of training for it. His team has not won a lot of games this year but hopefully they will improve in the future.

We continue to go camping with our RV, to Mount Kidd, and have found a new site we like in Kimberley, B.C. This will be our third year going there. Our grandson joined us there last year and hopefully will again this year. He loves riding his bike and is usually gone all day when with us. He has the ability to make friends at the campgrounds wherever we go.

My younger sister and her granddaughter have been joining us on different occasions in her mini camper. Her son (my godson) and his family join us occasionally.

This book is dedicated to my family and friends who gave me support and strength during hard times to go forward and achieve my goal/goals.

In spite of all the hardships I had to endure, I look back on my life and feel satisfied. I am still healthy at the age of 73. I spent 47 years in the workforce and was able to travel seeing a lot Canada, USA and abroad. I also was able to enjoy many good times with family and friends.

After reading many novels through the years I was encouraged and took interest in writing. I also completed a business writing course years ago. One of my goals was to write a book one day about my experiences and I have accomplished that task.

As Pearl Bailey once said; "You never find yourself until you face the truth".